Leland & Jacqueline Bolt

Family, History & Travels

Leland Emet Bolt, Sr

AuthorHouse™
1663 Liberty Drive
Bloomington, IN 47403
www.authorhouse.com
Phone: 833-262-8899

Because of the dynamic nature of the Internet, any web addresses or links contained in this book may have changed
since publication and may no longer be valid. The views expressed in this work are solely those of the author and do not
necessarily reflect the views of the publisher, and the publisher hereby disclaims any responsibility for them.

Any people depicted in stock imagery provided by Getty Images are models,
and such images are being used for illustrative purposes only.
Certain stock imagery © Getty Images.

This book is printed on acid-free paper.

ISBN: 978-1-6655-4801-4 (sc)
ISBN: 978-1-6655-4802-1 (e)

Library of Congress Control Number: 2021925835

Print information available on the last page.

Published by AuthorHouse 01/20/2022

CHAPTER 1

The Meeting

When the US Naval Academy (USNA) class of 1951 completed their third year, they were assigned for two months to ships of the fleet as junior officers under instruction. Leland "Lee" Bolt, Tom McCreless, Bob Carius, and Dana Estes were assigned to USS Charles P. Cecil (DDR-835) homeported in Newport, Rhode Island.

The Midshipmen did not receive much money, perhaps $78 per month. The Torpedo Station, then on Goat Island, had a twelve-cent movie theater, and drinks at the officers' club were cheap. One evening, Tom McCreless and Lee were at the club talking to Kay Goodwin, wife of the Torpedo Station Commanding Officer. She said a sister of the Executive Officer's wife, Jacqueline Barker, was visiting from Florida. Tom called and got a date with her. Lee later dated her, and they toured the famous estates and palatial homes on bicycles. The most prominent was the Breakers, the Vanderbilt estate at 44 Ochre Point Avenue. Can you believe fresh or salt water, hot or cold! The next day when Lee called, Jacqueline's sister, Hazel, said he'd made her do too much, and she was soaking her legs in the tub.

Lee met the Torpedo Station Executive Officer (XO), Captain Lucas, and Hazel, and was entertained at their Quarters 2 home.

1. The meeting in Newport, Rhode Island

Before his time was up on the destroyer, Lee knew Jacqueline was the girl for him. He sneaked away to visit her once, and the Lucases had him come for Christmas1950, instead of going home to Idaho. He was able to find a miniature USNA class of 1951 ring and have a tourmaline mounted. He presented the ring and asked Jacqueline to marry him. She said she was already engaged to someone else, and Lee said, "You are not married yet." She accepted the ring.

Lee slipped away a couple more times to visit Jacqueline. She came to his USNA graduation in June 1951 and met his parents. It was a great graduation, with parades, the traditional throwing of the caps and girlfriend or parents helping change their uniforms to Commissioned Officers. Lee's orders were to report to the Amphibious Warfare School in San Diego and upon completion of courses report to USS *Lenawee* (APA-195) in the Western Pacific.

2. Sailing on the Chesapeake Bay

Jacqueline and Lee went to New York City, got rooms at the Roosevelt Hotel, and saw a couple of Broadway shows. She then returned to her job at the Naval War College in Newport, and Lee flew to meet his parents in Chicago, drive them home, and report to the school in San Diego. He completed his courses and reported aboard *Lenawee* in Sasebo, Japan.

CHAPTER 2

The Wedding

Upon his return to San Diego in November 1951, Lee sent Jacqueline a telegram saying, "I'm here awaiting your arrival." Jacqueline came and got a San Diego apartment. She had various jobs, first as receptionist at an auto painting shop, then a clerk for a CPA, and then Secretary at an automobile dealership.

3. Jacqueline's San Diego apartment

By June 1952, Lee was able to get leave for the wedding. Jacqueline was one of nine children, and her parents could not host the wedding. Lee's mother was happy to have it at the Emmett, Idaho, St. Mary's Church, where Lee had been baptized and confirmed. Jacqueline called the Episcopal Bishop of Idaho, Frank Rhea, asking him to marry them at the Emmett Church. He said it would be better if she called the vicar, Father Ashton, first. Both agreed.

Lee's mother, Fern, arranged for Lee's uncle, Kenneth Denman, to give the bride away. Ken, being an attorney, called Jacqueline's mother to ensure that the family consented. Lee's high school classmate, Ensign Donald Buck, who had just graduated from USNA, was home on leave and served as best man. Lee's USNA classmate, Ensign Francis J. Degnan, and his wife, Eleanor, were on change-of-duty orders, and he was an usher. It was a rare military wedding in Emmett, Idaho. The Bolts' neighbors, the Calenders, had the reception at their home next door to Lee's parents.

4. Wedding at St. Mary's Church in Emmett, Idaho

The wedding night was in the bridal suite of the Hotel Boise, compliments of Jesse and Bob Naylor, longtime friends of the Bolts. Jesse was a daughter of Andrew Little, and a principal manager in the family sheep and cattle business.

The couple went on to Sun Valley Idaho for a couple of days and then north to Stanley and over the mountains to Warm Lake. Winter tree falls had just been cut by the US Forest Service. It was a rainy, cold night, so they got a cabin at Warm Lake. Heat and hot water had to be provided by a wood stove, which they had to start. They had their first disagreement when Jacqueline told Lee he did not know how to build a fire.

5. Jacqueline and the couple's car in Haley, Idaho

The next day, they went on to Cascade and the Bolt cabin in McCall, Idaho, where they stayed a few days. The Bolt cabin was comfortable and near the beach. The old Brown Tie and Lumber Company mill was there, and they got a tour. Lee reminisced that, in the old days, big blocks of ice were cut from the frozen lake in winter and stored in sawdust-insulated buildings for summer use. In the sawdust, the blocks stayed frozen all summer.

Upon their return to Emmett late in the day, a host of friends shivareed the newlyweds, making them push each other about four blocks down Main Street. Attempts to escape were unsuccessful. Then they were told to produce strong drink, or she would go to Fruitland, twenty miles south, and he to Pearl, about thirty miles north. Lee remembered a bottle of Champagne stored at his parents' house, so he poured each a shot glass full. They had not said how much!

A few days later, the newlyweds departed for San Diego, but their car had a universal joint failure in Lovelock, Nevada. They remained to await the new parts, which did not come for three days. They were repacking to leave when the lights went out. Checking with the Motel, they found that lights out at midnight was standard practice. With borrowed battery-driven lights, they finished packing.

The next day, they boarded the bus and went to the Lankershim Hotel in Los Angeles. The next morning, Jacqueline took the bus to her San Diego apartment, and Lee flew to Hawaii to report aboard *Lenawee.*

CHAPTER 3

Ship Overhaul in Hawaii

Lenawee had sailed to Hawaii to begin a three-month overhaul in the Pearl Harbor Navy Shipyard. After lots of phone calls, it was decided that Jacqueline could come to the island. Lee found a little motel-type cottage in Kailua and rented a car to meet her at the airport. It was a bright little place, and Lee could ride with Dave Keiser to and from work. Once or twice, children came to their door and asked if they wanted to come to a luau. If they did not go, the kids brought food. Jacqueline could keep up her tennis game by playing at the officers' club, which was then nearby on Kailua's North Coast Drive.

Jacqueline and Lee met his father's college girlfriend, Bess Keebler, who was living in the heart of the Waikiki district.

6. The young couple meet the college girlfriend of Leland's father in Waikiki

In Wahiawa they found the Tanoye family of Lee's father's foreman, Herb, who supervised workers on the fruit farms. Herb and his wife and son had been living in California. World War II had imposed the law that people of Japanese descent, citizen or not, could not live within two hundred miles of the Pacific coast. Lee's father had helped Herb and many more of these internees find employment farther inland. Mrs. Tanoye was so excited to see Lee and Jacqueline and kept exclaiming that Herb was her firstborn. The family took Lee and Jacqueline to a memorable feast at the Pearl City Tavern. There was a great stage show too.

7. Jacqueline on the couple's patio chair in Kailua

Lee and Jacqueline later found a small condominium in the Waikiki district, near Fort DeRussy. Lee could ride with shipmates to and from the ship. They still had no car. But Jackie had a lot of beach time and observed the Hawaiians climbing the trees and cutting loose the coconuts in husk, making a big *thud*.

They had lots of fun in that popular beach tourist area. At the time, there were only four hotels in Waikiki—The Royal Hawaiian; Moana; Surfrider; and Halekulani, which had simple cottages on the beach. Also, they could watch the Matson liners and other passenger ships arrive and leave from the Aloha Tower pier. Girls brought leis and danced to welcome the passengers or see them off.

CHAPTER 4

Back in San Diego

When the couple arrived back in San Diego, it was obvious that they would soon have a child, and their rental management advised that children were not permitted. They looked for weeks, all over San Diego and nearby communities, but found no place that allowed children. You could have dogs or cats, even snakes, but no kids. Lee's father told them to see what they could buy.

They found an eight hundred-square-foot two-bedroom, one-bath house at 3537 Boundary Street, with a big fenced-in backyard. They did not have the $3,500 down payment—that was far more than their annual household income! Lee's parents loaned them the money, and they registered a second trust deed to his parents.

Their first son was born April 13, 1953, at the Naval Air Station North Island (NASNI) in Coronado, California. Lee had been deployed to the Far East again, but Jacqueline got a phone hookup to the ship in Hong Kong to tell him he was a daddy. Jacque Burgess, the wife of Lee's shipmate, Andy Burgess, had taken her for a checkup, and the baby was born. The baby lost a bit of weight, so they could not go home for a couple of days. Jacque had her infant son, Andy Jr., but was still wonderfully able to be there for Jacqueline and the baby.

The NASNI Dispensary was pressing Jacqueline to name the baby and said she must name him before they would be allowed to go home. Alone, she decided he would be named after his daddy, as Leland Emet Bolt Jr.

8. Lee Jr. and his mother in 1953

The wives of Navy and Marine Corps personnel helped one another. Some, such as Doris Catalano and Claire Hutchison, were wives of Lee's USNA classmates. Others were wives whose husbands were aboard *Lenawee*, including Jacque Burgess and Dottie Hale.

With an infant and alone, Jacqueline was helped a lot by the neighbors, the Crottses, and their daughters, Gay and Joy. Lee's parents came for a short time to help but had to return to the ripening fruit farm and packinghouse.

The Boundary Street house was ideal, close to good shopping in North Park, and Chris's Market was in the same block. The large fenced-in backyard gave privacy and lots of room for sunning. Jacqueline had light olive skin that got darker with sun. Lee Jr. had that skin that got brown, because she put the little guy in the sun for short times. Daddy was Leland or Lee, so they began calling the baby Brownie, and the nickname lasted.

In 1953, when Lee was again at sea, Jacqueline took Brownie to Idaho to visit the grandparents and then by train to Omaha, Nebraska, where Captain Lucas and Jacqueline's sister, Hazel, were then stationed. It was a remarkable train trip. An attendant would sit in the compartment with the baby while she went to the dining car. At one point, the car was detached from the train to await another train that attached it and went on to Omaha

9. Jacqueline and Navy friends in Omaha

Captain Lucas was Commander of the Naval Personnel Center, Omaha. He and Hazel wonderfully entertained Jacqueline with their friends, and Hazel was always a great hostess.

The train trip back to Idaho was equally enjoyable.

Lee had been relieved of *Lenawee* duties by September 1953, but was ordered to Shore Patrol Headquarters in San Diego for a few weeks. He reported for work at 6:00 p.m. and got off at 3:00 a.m. Jacqueline would welcome him and ask what had gone on. He'd relate stories for another hour or so before they went to bed.

One story was about a phone call from the wife of an enlisted man, who said she was being beaten by him. Lee had been warned of this kind of situation, but she agreed to sign a complaint. The Shore Patrol got San Diego Police to assist. Once they had him in the "paddy wagon," she refused to sign the complaint, and he was released.

Another time, the phone man said it was a captain, who was angry. Lee took the call and learned it was Captain Bill Hutchison USMC, a USNA classmate. Shore Patrol chased the escapee but lost him around Temecula.

CHAPTER 5

USS Princeton (CVA-37 then CVS-37)

In November 1953, Lee reported to the aircraft carrier USS *Princeton* (CVA-37), homeported in San Diego. He was Boiler Officer, which included fuel and water systems. *Princeton* was scheduled for a five-month overhaul at Naval Shipyard Bremerton, Washington. Lee's father and mother helped Jacqueline and Brownie get there and assisted in making a home. Lee and his father got a crib at a secondhand store, but it fell apart. The baby was unharmed, and Lee glued it solidly together.

Soon after the parents departed, Jacqueline called the landlord about the heating system; it was a cold winter. The landlord asked about the fuel gauge. Jacqueline had never had a fuel oil heater, but the tank was filled, and all was well.

The Bolt rental was next door to *Princeton* Damage Control Assistant Roy Huettel and his wife, Merle. They were extremely helpful, and Jacqueline was going to be a mother again in five months.

As *Princeton* was completing overhaul, Lee was able to take a few days off to pack the car and take Jacqueline and Brownie to the grandparents in Idaho. Merle Huettel, watching them pack, saw Jacqueline and said they were the most disorganized family she had ever seen. She said, "Lee goes out and packs items into the car, but Jaqueline gets things and takes them back in the house."

While at the grandparents' home, they had Brownie's first birthday cake. The grandparents took mother and baby back to San Diego.

10. Brownie's first birthday cake

Lee returned to *Princeton* (now CVS-37) to complete the overhaul. Jacqueline went to the NAS North Island for a regular checkup, and Jon Warner Bolt was born on May Day 1954. She just had babies in about 8 months. NAS North Island was supposed to just do birth check-ups. Babies were supposed to be born at the Naval Hospital, not far away in San Diego

This time, Lee and Jacqueline had discussed the name for the coming baby. There had been newspaper funnies in the 1930s and '40s titled *Alley Oop*. Alley was a caveman who rode a dinosaur named Dinney. Later, a Doctor One Mug entered the scene and invented a time machine that would bring Alley Oop and other ancient characters into the twentieth century. Dr. One Mug's assistant was named Jon. They chose it as the new baby's first name. His middle name, Warner, was chosen because Lee's great grandparents, the Zimmermans, had been friends of the Pop Warner football family from New York.

Lee got off *Princeton* for a few days to see the baby and help, but had to return for the sail to San Diego. Again, the baby's weight dropped, and there was a wait until they could go home. Jacqueline's sister, Nelva Deane, came to help with the two boys. She stayed several months and attended Hoover High School with the neighbor girls, Gay and Joy Crotts.

Lee and Jacqueline found that Ray and Shirley Nichols (his friends from Idaho) had moved to San Diego. He was an insurance adjuster, and she was a waitress at Bali Hai restaurant. They had three boys at the time, and there were many good times with the Bolts.

Jacqueline made a great home at 3537 Boundary Street. She enjoyed sunning in the yard. The boys could wander all around but not get out of the secure yard. Lee did barbecues with Bert Crotts showing him how to do a full-size fish and seasoning techniques.

11. Jacqueline sunning in the yard

Incredibly, they had not met their neighbors to the south. The Bolts sent a box of apples, and nobody was home, so the apples were left with the Brooks. Good thing, because they had a boy and a girl about the age of the Bolt boys. Grover Brooks was from the Southwestern Idaho and Eastern Oregon area, where Lee was raised. There were reciprocal birthday parties and lots of beach time. Mr. Brooks had been working for Morrison Knudsen

Company on Wake Island in 1941. He was taken prisoner and spent the entire war in a Japanese prison camp. After the war he was working in Morocco, where he met and married the French girl, Madelaine.

Now with two boys, Jacqueline had her sister to help. Days were full of rinsing out cloth diapers and washing them in the machine. The Bolt grandparents visited in winters.

12. Jacqueline with both boys

CHAPTER 6

Fleet Gunnery School San Diego

Lee left *Princeton* and reported to Fleet Gunnery School, San Diego, in 1956. After completing the instructor training course, he taught officer courses. All officers, except the Commanding Officer and Lee, were "Mustangs" (enlisted personnel who rose through ranks and gained officer commissions). It was a great group that worked and played hard.

In March 1956, Lee was promoted to LT USN, and it was customary for the promoted officer to have a "wetting down" party for fellow officers and wives. Lee and Jacqueline minimized the wetting down party cost by making their own snacks, serving artillery punch as a single drink, and having the party in the large backyard at their Boundary Street home.

13. The new lieutenant and boys, 1956

After the combining of military services under the Defense Department, units were not permitted to have Navy Day celebrations extending into the community. The Navy Department arranged local on-base observances. A stage play was developed, titled *The Spirit of the Navy*, written by noted Hollywood writer John Ford. It featured many historical Navy events, such as Admiral Perry opening Japan to trading and Marine Corps battle for Guadalcanal. Lee was selected to play John Paul Jones in the San Diego production, staged at Naval Training Center San Diego Auditorium. This event was Captain John Paul Jones arranging the exchange of gun salutes with the French Admiral in a French port of call. For his performance, Lee received a November 21, 1956, letter of appreciation from the Chief of Naval Operations (CNO).

Jacqueline was still taking Lee to work each morning at the Gunnery School, driving from North Park down Wabash Street (later I-15) and picking him up after 4:00 p.m. The light heavyweight boxing champion, Archie Moore, had a home near Ocean Boulevard with a swimming pool in the shape of a boxing glove. The boys were always excited to point out Archie's home. One day they had a special thrill, meeting Mr. and Mrs. Archie Moore in a market near his home. Lee later met Archie on an airplane and had a visit about Archie's venture into heavy weight class. That section of I-15 is now named for Archie Moore.

Realizing the coming of nuclear propulsion, Lee took a course in nuclear physics at San Diego State University (SDSU). When using a borrowed power lawn mower, the cord caught and beat up his leg. He was on crutches for a month or so, and Jacqueline had to drive him to and from the Gunnery School and the course at SDSU.

Jaqueline gave birth on January 2, 1957, to their daughter, Carmen Loree Bolt, who died January 8 at Naval Hospital, San Diego. She is interred in San Diego's Mount Hope Cemetery.

CHAPTER 7

USS Uhlmann (DD-687)

Lee was detached from the Gunnery School in March 1958 and ordered as operations officer, USS *Uhlmann* (DD-687). Jacqueline took him to the Naval Air Station North Island passenger terminal, from which he flew to Yokosuka, Japan. As soon as these orders had been received, the wife of the officer Lee was to relieve called to find out when he would relieve her husband, Hank Marbot. There was much to do before he could leave, because by this time, he was the school's Training Officer. Mrs. Marbot kept calling for weeks, because, even after being relieved at the school, reporting to *Uhlmann* dragged on because of tight security operations.

Another problem was that a sailor, apparently at the passenger center at NAS North Island showed up at the Boundary Street door, telling Jacqueline that Lee had asked him to take care of her. What a shock! She called Ray and Shirley Nichols and communicated the situation to Gunnery School Commanding Officer, now Captain Ensey. Ray and his older son came and stayed with Jacqueline for a few evenings in case the guy returned. These were two big guys, and he never returned.

Lee finally boarded the ship at White Beach in Okinawa, where the ship's boat picked him up in beach surf. He had to wade through surf to board the boat. He became USS *Uhlmann* (DD-687) Operations Officer and Navigator, and Hank's wife stopped calling Jacqueline! It was unusual for the Operations Officer to also be the Navigator. The Executive Officer was usually the Navigator and would assume command if anything happened to the Commanding Officer. Uhlmann Executive Officer was not qualified for command, so if anything happened to the CO, Lee would have been in command.

After the ship arrived back in San Diego, there was crew leave and a few duty changes, followed by ship preparations for a board of inspection and survey, preliminary to a shipyard overhaul.

At one of the preparatory meetings, a message came that Lee's son, Brownie, had been hit by a car. Captain Erikson said, "Go," and Lee was on his way. Brownie had been walking home from kindergarten (they could still do it then) in Halloween costume. At an intersection, a car had hit him. After naval hospital examinations, no major damage was found, only minor scratches and bruises.

Lee and Jacqueline made the customary call on the Captain and his wife. It was a great evening, and they got to meet the pet turtle, who came tapping at the patio door.

Lee's relief, LT Ping, reported aboard and soon became Operations Officer and Navigator. Lee departed November 14, 1958. His unused leave provided income for a short time, but he needed a job. He knew General Dynamics Astronautics and others were hiring and turned in requests to do anything they needed.

A friend counseled that you had to identify the job you were seeking, and they didn't often look for employees in the "anything" folder." He changed his request to "engineering administration" and got a job, reporting in late January 1959. Hours were spent on security briefings and training.

When he finally got to his department, the supervisor said, "Where have you been?" and advised he was to be scheduling and monitoring engineering for support equipment to be installed at InterContinental Ballistic Missile (ICBM) bases all over the country, and he was far behind in the job!

One day, Jacqueline had the two boys in their 1958 Volkswagen convertible and was shopping near El Cajon, when it rained and the convertible top leaked. She drove to a Volkswagen dealership and said they should buy the car. They would not meet her price, so she stayed. The boys were inquisitive and all around the place. Finally, they purchased it, and Jacqueline had to call Shirley Nichols to take her home.

Pete and Anna Guerrero lived across Boundary Street from the Bolts, and Anna sometimes helped with the two boys. Anna had a tiny baby girl, and the boys were watching her change diapers. Brownie said, "Looks like a taco". Then Anna told them how babies were made, and Jon said, "Oh, no. My mommy can't open her mouth that wide."

The six blocks of Boundary Street in the vicinity was eighteen feet wide, with two-way traffic and parking on one side. Lee carried a petition to homeowners to make it one way. Each evening, he went to get signers and met many people, and often their pets (among them an ocelot). Only two didn't sign. The city made it one way and thanked Lee for the petition.

On August 11, 1959, Lee got an afternoon call from Shirley Nichols, saying Jaqueline was having pains and driving to the hospital, and she had Brownie and Jon. Lee asked why she'd let her go alone. She had tried but could not stop her. Lee got to Sharp Memorial Hospital in time to see Jacqueline going up in the elevator. There were several times of pains and having Lee wait outside while they checked her condition.

Then Stuart Clay Bolt was her best birthday present ever. Lee and Jacqueline had planned his name too. Jacqueline's family was from Florida, and the Bolts originated in Virginia. General Robert E. Lee's outstanding scouting and intelligence leader was J. E. B. (Jeb) Stuart, and Jacqueline liked the name Clay, perhaps for Henry Clay of Revolutionary fame.

While Lee was at work, Jacqueline was ensuring the boys got more training for their lives to come. Since Daddy was in the navy, she had them in swimming lessons twice a week, and between times, there were tap dance lessons. First it was Brownie and Jon, but Clay later got the training. Boys needed to be strong swimmers and dancers!

CHAPTER 8

Poway, the Little Country Village

The little house on Boundary Street was small for this family of five. Lee and Jacqueline looked for something bigger. Lee was working at General Dynamics Astronautics with Paul Neuenswander, who lived in Poway, which was a small rural community North of San Diego. Paul said his brother-in-law had a lot on Putney Road that he might sell and the Bolts build a home.

Lee and Jacqueline found that their friend Ray Nichols was "moonlighting" selling standard on-your-lot homes, and they found one they liked. They modified it to make the garage a living room and built an attached two-car garage and breezeway on the other side. Paul's brother who sold them the lot was a mason and contracted to build a fireplace in the living room. Mr. Rollins was a friend and Poway dirt-moving guy, who they contracted to prepare the lot. Then, since there was no city sewer system, they had to put in a septic tank and leach line system. But there was plenty of room on this three-quarter acre lot. There was city electrical service, but no gas service, so a propane tank and pump system were added.

In May 1960, the boys completed school, and the Bolts moved to 13802 Putney Road in Poway. Soon, a hot dining room floor revealed a hot water leak under the floor, causing a messy rework.

14. The new Poway home had more room.

They were able to sell the Boundary Street property but made the mistake of accepting a two-on-one rental property on Van Dyke Street as part of the deal. The boys hated having to work at the rentals, particularly after one of the occupants trashed the place. Within a year, they sold the rentals.

Inspection required rework of the septic tank system. There was lots of landscaping to do, like embankments and driveway paving.

Brownie and Jon were able to start school (second and first grades) in September.

In June 1960, Lee became a member of the first Lions Club of Poway and their first "tail twister." Lee and Jacqueline found many new friends in Poway. Lee helped start the new St. Bartholomew's Episcopal Church, serving as Treasurer and acolyte until others could be recruited. At first, church was in a store building in the old Midland Road shopping center, and then it was held in a vacant home at the intersection of Espola and Twin Peaks Roads.

Raymond and Shirley Nichols found a big lot in Lakeside and built one of the on-your-lot houses he was selling. It was on Los Coaches Road. They were close with the Bolt family, because they had children the same age and they had known Lee back in Emmett, Idaho.

With the two older boys in school, Jacqueline took Clay all kinds of places, like to Tijuana for haircuts, to the hairdresser, shopping, and out to lunch. Sometimes they visited friends, like the Nichols in Lakeside or others in San Diego. Each morning Clay asked, "Where are we going today, Mommy?"

Lee joined the USS *Wiseman* (DE-667) Reserve Crew as LT U. S. Naval Reserve (USNR) and became Executive Officer in June 1961. By this time, they had bought Bert Crotts's 1948 Plymouth, and Lee was no longer dependent on Jacqueline to take and retrieve him from work.

The family went to Idaho for a vacation with the Bolt grandparents at their summer cabin in McCall. Special delivery orders were received that *Wiseman* and other Naval Reserve ships were recalled to active duty by President Kennedy for the Berlin Crisis. The family returned to San Diego, where Lee checked out at General Dynamics Astronautics and became Executive Officer USS *Wiseman* (DE667), with a promotion to Lieutenant Commander (LCDR) USNR.

The next three months were filled with ship upgrades, repair, and readiness exercises for deployment. In January 1962, the recalled ships departed for the Philippines and Vietnam.

Wiseman Commanding Officer's wife, Dorothy, and Jacqueline (now Executive Officer's wife) helped get support for families of the hundred recalled reserve personnel who had left other jobs for an estimated six-month deployment. One day, Lee got a rather cool letter from Jacqueline about the retaining landscaping on the lower bank of their house giving way in the rain, with mud running down to the Munn's back door. She had been shoveling at midnight.

Jacqueline kept the boys busy and ensured they did their homework. She had help from friends and neighbors, like the Neuenswanders, Herrs, Hefleys and Nicholses.

When *Wiseman* was returning from deployment, Jacqueline and Dorothy came to Hawaii and met the ship for a few days before their return. It was a joyous time, just as it was every time they could spend days in that tropical paradise. Brownie and Clay stayed with the Nichols family, and Jon went to Anaheim to stay with Jacqueline's brother Bill's family. He got to play cap league baseball and really liked it.

CHAPTER 9

General Dynamics and the Naval Reserve

Back in San Diego in September 1962, *Wiseman* was returned to Reserve Status, and Lee became the Commanding Officer.

Lee's former employer, General Dynamics Astronautics, had combined into General Dynamics Convair (GDC). His old department no longer existed, so he was assigned to work in the Systems Analysis group. Jacqueline became a member of the Convair Recreation Association and started playing tennis again.

Jacqueline had Brownie and Jon in a Cub Scout den and helped the den mother with their training. For a time, Lee agreed to be pack chairman, and they staged events such as a Soap Box Derby.

The Poway School Board was overwhelmed by this little rural community's sudden population influx, leading to huge demands for more teachers and facilities. They looked for someone to just run it, and they found him. Lee and Jacqueline knew him but had no idea he could bring about such deficient schools. There was no need for Poway students to attend classes; they just had to pass examinations. Truancy officers would see kids at the beach during school hours, and they were on the Poway plan!

Jon, in second grade, brought home a report card with an A in mathematics, but a note in the remarks said he was having difficulty in mathematics. Lee brought this to a school board and PTA meeting and got no satisfactory answers.

Jacqueline met with his teacher, and all his papers had April misspelled. The teacher said she did not want to disappoint him. Jacqueline asked how he could learn if she allowed him to get it wrong and assured her, we corrected that sort of thing at home. Jacqueline told her she was not even a good babysitter.

That teacher got tenure, and they found out why when a man with the same surname from the County Superintendent's office came to address the PTA—her husband!

Lee and Jacqueline became active in the Poway Young Republicans organization. Lee was Chairman, and Jaqueline worked their precinct. It was 1964 and Jacqueline just missed winning her precinct voting for Barry Goldwater. She could have had a majority for Republicans but a few saw the TV news that Goldwater would not win. Our absentees did not vote!

15. The Poway Young Republicans

Beginning in 1960 with gunnery school friends, they had lots of fun in Tijuana, Mexico. It began with Jai Alai games at Fronton Palacio and dinner at Mr. Angel's restaurant for great steak and delicious salads. Poway had limited dining options, so Jacqueline and Lee often went to Tijuana for dinner, leaving the boys with Mrs. Armstrong. They loved her place, and if they were asleep when the parents came home, Mrs. Armstrong would suggest the boys stay and get picked up in the morning.

Lee began taking Brownie and Jon to St. Bartholomew's Episcopal Church, which was being organized, with a visiting priest each week. Lee filled in as a teacher and acolyte and then became Treasurer. But he and Jacqueline decided it would be better to attend church as a family. Jacqueline's family were Baptists, and Lee was an Episcopalian. The Nuenswanders lived on the same block, and they met the Herrs and Hefleys, so the Bolts went to the Christian and Missionary Alliance Church.

It was very small, so the congregation had to help maintain the church and grounds. One big yard maintenance work event included a birthday, the plan for which was to have cake and congratulations after work. Going to get the cake from the seat in the car, Lee found that the retired minister, Reverend Degrote, had gotten tired and rested in that seat. Lee remembered the reverend sitting there and Brownie looking at the smashed cake and saying, "Yes, Reverend Degrote."

Jacqueline became Church Treasurer.

The church had a boys' brigade, like the Boy Scouts, but it demanded lots of participation by fathers. There was hiking and camping trips, for which Ervin Herr made great stews. On one occasion, they were camped in a forest site. It was getting dark, and the boys were getting sleeping bags ready. Rodney Herr, Brownie, and Jon were placing the beds at the edge of their area, close to some Marines who had been drinking. Lee did not like the conversation and asked them to leave the boys alone.

They asked, "Who said that?"

It was a bit dark, so five foot six, 136-pound Lee held up his sleeping bag to look bigger. He told them, "I said that." It was tense for a moment, but they retired to their camp.

Jacqueline began fitness training at the Convair Recreation Association (CRA) and played tennis more often.

16. Jacqueline, the Foleys, and Herb Zohrer in Monterey

27

Lee's employer, General Dynamics, arranged annual employees' nights at Disneyland. For a reasonable entry fee, all rides were free. In the process, the Bolts visited Jacqueline's brother Bill and family in Anaheim. They still got together with them after they moved the family to Hawthorne, California.

Lee helped Clay and a friend build a rocket and test-fly it in a Poway field.

Lee's boss, Don Frederickson, had wrestled as a young student. He suggested the boys could benefit from this one-on-one sport. Lee had wrestled at the Naval Academy. La Mesa Recreation Wrestling Coach Bill Clauder had a great reputation and was later a 2002 inductee to the California State Wrestling Hall of Fame. Lee and Don took their sons to La Mesa for training. They worked on their business projects while the boys were in training. The trainees wrestled other recreation centers at competitive meets in and near the San Diego area.

17. Mommy and her boys on a trip to Idaho

About 1966, Jacqueline was impaneled on a San Diego Superior Court jury homicide case. It was alleged that the defendant entered a resale store downtown and demanded all the cash from an owner at the register. The co-owner had heard noise and called out. The defendant allegedly killed the one at the cash register and hunted through the store for the other owner.

The jury continued deliberations but was unable to get a unanimous vote. Lee had to get fresh clothing to Jacqueline at the motel where they were sequestered. Finally, Jacqueline turned to the woman not voting for conviction and said, "You lied to the judge. You said you were not opposed to the death penalty. This could be a death penalty case, and you refuse to accept it."

The woman made the vote unanimous. The defendant lived for more than twenty-five years on death row.

CHAPTER 10

The Return to San Diego

The Poway school system only got worse. Lee and Jacqueline were always on the road back to town for Lee's Navy obligations and for beach time with friends. They decided to return to San Diego. At the first showing of their home, Jacqueline had a fire in the fireplace and a sweet-smelling cake in the oven. The first people through the door bought it. But school was not out yet, so the realtor found a house on Powers Road near the Herrs and Hefleys until school was out. They knew they wanted to live in the Kensington neighborhood of San Diego but could not afford those for sale. They rented a home in the area until Jacqueline found a home she liked and they could afford. The kids started school, and it was not long until a home in their price range became available. They moved for the third time in a year to 5155 Canterbury Drive.

Brownie and Jon got into model airplanes. Brownie made gliders, and Jon made rubber band and engine-powered planes. Jon built a controller to direct planes in takeoff, flight, and landing.

Brownie started playing drums and wound up with a full set, bought with a loan from Daddy. Thankfully, most practices were at the home of the Bridges, well off the neighborhood's area of dense homes. He delivered a small newspaper to repay the drum loan and quit the minute it was paid!

Jon took up wind instruments, playing the trumpet and French horn.

Brownie was on the Hoover wrestling team in high school, and Jon ran cross-country and was a pole vaulter. He learned the art of bending the pole, and Lee helped by catching the pole in practice sessions.

Jon had a *Union Tribune* delivery route for a time and gave it to Clay. It was officially Jon's because Clay was underage. He had to learn a lot, beginning with simple laws of physics, like when he took too many papers from one side of the front basket. They spilled! Lee came to the rescue and discouraged Clay from giving up.

He went on to deliver morning papers until graduation from High School in 1977. By that time, he had saved enough money to buy a new Honda Accord. The salesman called his friends to see the kid who paid cash for a new car!

The Bolt boys took to motorcycles in the 1960s. Jon bought an old Maico and rode it for a while, until it failed. Brownie fixed it well enough to sell. Lee had a Chevrolet pickup truck into which they loaded motorcycles (theirs and Rod Herr's), plus sleeping bags.

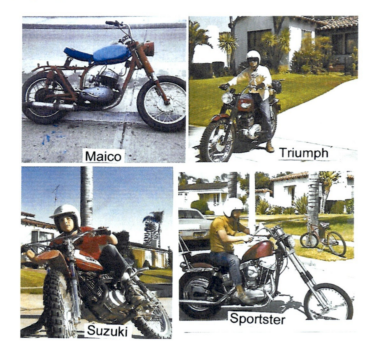

18. The Bolts rode motorcycles

Lee added food and other living necessities, and they were off to the mountains or Salton Sea. Clay had an old Honda 80 and then progressed onto a Suzuki. Lee used the Honda 80 for training Clay and then tried to keep up with them on the trails.

Brownie bought a Harley Davidson 900cc Sportster in a basket. All the parts were found to be there, and in some cases, there were extras. He sorted out all the parts and gave Jacqueline daily assignments to get the damaged parts fixed and chromed where necessary. Though he had no instructions, he assembled the cycle and took it on a proof run. Then he rode it a thousand miles to Idaho to show to the grandparents. About Winnemucca, Nevada, he was tired, and it was late. He had little money left, so he called Jacqueline to have her assure the motel of payment.

Clay followed his brothers taking wrestling lessons at La Mesa recreation, and played goalie on the Hoover high school soccer team.

The boys had various science fair projects. Though they were good, none won the big prizes. Jon built an electric power decision maker that could be biased toward either yes or no. He also built a model airplane remote control unit. Brownie did a demonstration of plants' power to absorb and draw water up to upper leaves and branches. Clay had a demonstration of urea used to treat sickle cell anemia.

Brownie graduated from Hoover High School in 1971 and attended Whittier College in California for a year

19. Brownie's high school graduation in 1971

Jon graduated from Hoover High School in 1972 and attended Mesa College in San Diego for a year.

20. Jon's high school graduation in 1972

With the older boys graduating, Jacqueline played more tennis at the CRA courts. She also kept in shape working out in the CRA fitness center. Over the late 1970s and into the 1990s, she won many trophies, mostly playing men, who dominated the tennis club.

21. Jacqueline won many trophies playing mostly men

In April 1972 CAPT Nelson, Lee's former Commander of the Destroyer Division, called to say he was night duty officer at CINCPACFLT Headquarters at Pearl Harbor, and they needed a relief. Lee got permission from GDC and began active duty at CINCPACFLT 28 May 1972. As night duty officer in ADM Nimitz's old headquarters war room, Lee was CINCPACFLT 20:00 to 08:00, with one day on and 2 days off. He could call any staff officer, but his team had to brief all the Admirals in the morning, and of course most of it was Viet Nam.

Lee was promoted to Captain, USNR 1 July 1972, and had a one-bedroom apartment at Macalapa, near the Command Center. Jacqueline came and they had a cottage at Fort DeRusy on Waikiki beach. Then CAPT Nelson and his wife had them live in their Makiki top floor condominium while they traveled. There was a great view of Waikiki and Diamond Head, but caring for the dog was included.

There were occasional staff parties. One Commander always brought his beautiful and provocatively dressed wife. All eyes had to see what she wore, and hopefully get in the conversation.

After his service as night duty officer at CINCPACFLT headquarters, Lee was ordered to two weeks active duty on a CINCPACFLT team for the annual South Korean Defense Exercise. Jacqueline did quick research and said she wanted a Korean smokey topaz ring. He flew to Pearl Harbor, where he met CAPT Caldwell and others of the group. At dinner with the Caldwells, he remembered that he had previously met the Captain's wife, Suzie, when she had dated Lee's Classmate (Harry Cooper) while at the Naval Academy.

The group flew to Seoul, Korea, and then by bus arrived at Camp Smith, where Lee was stationed, and on to Tegu Air Base with the others. At Camp Smith an Army Sergeant boarded the bus, asking "Where is that Navy Colonel?" Lee raised his hand, and they took him to his quarters. Again, he represented CINCPACFLT, but in Marine Greens, with black rank insignias.

Lee was called again to Navy active duty for five months in 1974 as a member of the DOD Total Force Study Group, under the Assistant Secretary for Manpower. The study surveyed world security threats and developed a DOD plan for the possible next wars. He had an apartment in Arlington, Virginia. Jacqueline visited him after taking care of the boys' transitions and home provisions.

On the return to San Diego, they stopped for Lee's parents' seventy-fifth wedding anniversary event in Boise, Idaho.

CHAPTER 11

The Boys in College

Brownie at Whittier College was within ninety miles of San Diego. He became famous for carving a key that would unlock the girls' dormitory. The next year, he transferred to Boise State University in Boise, Idaho. He qualified as an Idaho resident because of the time working on the Bolt farm in Emmett.

He then did not know what he wanted to do, but he made a great decision. He enlisted in the Army in 1975. After basic training, he was sent to Baylor University in Waco, Texas, for Laboratory Technician School. Then he was ordered to the Army Viral Research Laboratories at Ft. Dietrich, Maryland.

22. In the Army now

He cared for the animals and assisted the veterinarians in research. He found his calling and assisted one of the veterinarians in producing at least one technical paper. At the end of his enlistment, he went to the University of Idaho in Moscow and then to School of Veterinary Medicine at Washington State University in Pullman, Washington.

In 1975, Lee received his master's degree in systems management (MSSM) from University of Southern California (USC).

After taking community college courses, Jon transferred in 1975 to University of Idaho (U of I) in Moscow, Idaho.

Clay graduated from Hoover High school in 1977 and attended Community College in San Diego. He went on to University of California San Diego (UCSD) and graduated in 1981 from University of California San Francisco (UCSF) with a Doctorate in Pharmacy (PharmD).

Jon graduated from U of I in 1977, with a BS in Electrical Engineering and was hired by the disk memory division of Hewlett Packard Corporation in Cupertino, California. In a short time, he and Jerry Wurth led the move of the division to Boise, Idaho.

Jacqueline went to the family farm in 1978 and took her mother on a trip around Florida. They went to Key West and back through the East Coast and Cocoa, Florida where Jacqueline was born. They rented a riverboat and cruised on the Suwanee River.

Lee joined the GDC Tomahawk Navy cruise missile development program in 1978, becoming the manager of Support System Integration.

Jacqueline arranged a special lunch for Lee's fiftieth birthday at the Butcher Shop restaurant in Mission Valley. She rented a black Corvette and dressed as the sexy driver, arrived at Lee's office, and took him to the Butcher Shop. There the Boundary Street girls, Gay and Joy, joined them. The serving featured first-class dining and sexy waitresses. Afterward, Jacqueline returned Lee from lunch, where lots of the people were impressed with the service girl!

23. Lee's birthday was beautiful

The Bolts had a long history with Santa Clause. When Lee was in high school, a girlfriend's father had asked him to play Santa for his younger daughter, who was getting wise to him. He provided the costume, and the little girl had another year of make-believe. He continued playing Santa for many more years in Emmett, even while on leave from the Naval Academy.

After their marriage, Lee's mom made new Mr. and Mrs. Santa suits for Lee and Jacqueline. They even played Santa to the duty section of Lee's first ship, USS *Lenawee*, on Christmas 1952. Then they thrilled partygoers at their own boys' Christmas celebrations and were Santa and Mrs. Clause for their grandchildren and adult celebrations as well.

24. The Bolts were often Mr. and Mrs. Santa Clause

CHAPTER 12

The Party Times

During the 1970s through 1986, San Diego had annual Mummer's Day parades in Balboa Park. Participants featured gaudy and decorative costumes and accessories. The parade traced back to the mid-seventeenth century entertainment, blending elements from European and African heritage.

Jacqueline and Gay Woods first joined the parades in 1979. The parade was staged in Balboa Park. Entrants wore elaborate costumes and marched to music with theatrical instruments. In 1986, nobody obtained the parade permit, so participants were there without parade authorization. Jacqueline and Gay got a gaudy big tri-wheel biker to lead off and designated him the Grand Marshal. They showed the way for those present to have one final gaudy parade, and they were not bothered by the absence of a permit.

25. Jacqueline and Gay were Mummer's leaders

In 1980, Lee had been to Idaho to help his folks and saw Jon while there. A week or so after his return, Jon called to say he and Cherie Mabe were going to get married. Lee was surprised, which Jon detected, and said, "You seem surprised."

Lee said, "Yes. I was just there, and you were not even speaking to her."

Jon said, "Oh that. Well, we got together, and we do have similar objectives. And we're getting married May 1, 1980."

Cherie was from Lee's hometown (Emmett, Idaho), and he knew her father, who'd graduated from Emmett High School four years before him. It was a wonderful wedding at Boise's Plantation Country Club and Golf Course.

Brownie got his BS in Animal Science at U of I in 1983 and went on to Washington State University for his doctorate.

The mountain area north of San Diego, around Julian, had many apple orchards, and there was an Apple Festival each year. The Woods, Bolts, Woodwards, and Brooks bought a tree each year and had a party near their tree, along with plenty of champagne. The orchard owner pressed apples so the buyers could take home some cider.

26. Jacqueline and the apple tree

In 1982, Jacqueline and her sister, Hazel, took their mom for a tour of western national parks—Zion, Bryce, and Grand Canyon. Of course, they wound up in the Salt Lake City area and experienced the restrictions on liquor. Hazel and Jacqueline typically had a cocktail or wine with dinner. Ethel would not have any of that or even be near theirs! The State of Utah got into the act too. Jacqueline could go to the maître d'hôtel, who could sell liquor, and purchase wine. She brought it to the table, and the waitress brought wine glasses and ice. Ethel kept trying to get as far away from the booze as possible.

27. Mom and the girls toured national parks

In 1983, the British queen visited San Diego. The Bolts and friends went to the harbor to join in the royal welcoming festivities.

CHAPTER 13

Hawaii Became a Favorite

Trips to Hawaii became more frequent in 1982 and on, with grandchildren on Maui and, later, to Kauai and the Big Island (Hawaii). First, they would visit Lee's classmates on Oahu and then go to the other Islands.

28. Jacqueline, the Cromwells, the Bibbys, and Pappy Sears

Kilauea was erupting the day they landed at Hilo Airport in 1983. They had a spectacular view of the volcano spouting lava. Lee got an airplane to fly them by the eruption to experience the heat and turbulence. They liked that so much they did it at night!

After being tossed around a bit, they stayed at the Naniloa Surf Hotel. There was an earthquake while Lee was showering, and he almost had to flee naked. Fortunately, the shaking stopped before he exited the floor.

29. Flying over Kilauea's big eruption you could feel the heat!

Once, on the Kona side of the Big Island, a forest ranger asked Lee to babysit an orphan pig he had saved in the forest. Lee and Jacqueline agreed because plans were to rest around the pool that day. The baby pig slept close to Lee's feet and grunted when not sleeping. Best advice is do not babysit a little pig! Thankfully, the Ranger came about 4:00 p.m. and took his little pig. No more pig-sitting!

30. A baby boar to babysit

Lee photographed the eruptions from the ground as well, and the effects were seen all around the volcano. Roads and houses were destroyed.

31. Talk about road conditions!

The evening was warm and delightful, and the next morning, they were up and at the Hilo harbor fish auction. Fisherman sold the fish from the previous day's catch, and it was an interesting event, seeing how the buyers tested and evaluated the various fish offered. When on the Big Island, any visitor should go to the fish auction.

The next day, they went North from Hilo along the eastern coast and stopped at Akaka Falls. Then they went on to Honokaa, where Jacqueline's travel book indicated a good place to eat. It was good, and the sign said the place had rooms available, so they spent the night. The room was small and spartan, but clean and offered a sea view, and the cost was reasonable. However, everything in town closed at 9:00 PM!

32. Akaka Falls

The next day, they drove around the end of the island past the Parker Ranch and to that north point where King Kamehameha launched his canoes to invade other islands. Further around were beautiful gardens that Jacqueline loved dearly. Back in Kona and up the hill at Halualoa, she took haiku lei-making instruction.

33. Everywhere the beauty abounds

CHAPTER 14

Lots of San Diego Attractions and Travels

Jacqueline and Lee were adventuresome and visited lots of places in San Diego. They found the Redwing Bar on 30th street in North Park, where the Woods and Brooks often joined them.

34. Gay and Jacqueline at the Red Wing Bar

Once, they went to San Diego's Bill Miller Coliseum to see wrestling matches. This was a minimal venue in Logan Heights, where the bleachers were temporary. The wrestling was interesting, and they were among mostly black people.

As they were leaving, a man slipped and fell through an opening in the bleachers. Lee lent a helping hand, and the guy had a look of surprise when he saw the white hand. He took it with thanks!

Another place was a mud wrestling bar about 31st and El Cajon Boulevard. Some from the audience volunteered to wrestle with the girls in the huge mud basin.

In 1983, Lee had a business trip to the Atlas Missile launch sites at Cape Canaveral, and Jacqueline met him in Puerto Rico. They toured San Juan and took the primitive ferry boat to Louisa. The boat was drawn across the river by muscle power. A hawser leading from one side of the river to the other passed through spindles on the corners of the barge. The ramp was lowered and raised by chainfalls. Two big guys pulled the hawser through the spindles to cross the river.

Louisa was famous for masks fashioned from coconut shells, which they bought. They went to the rain forest on the western and southern coasts and visited the old fort in the walled area of town.

35. Jacqueline could always find a bar

In an old town bar, they sat next to an attorney, who asked Lee what they were drinking. Vodka and tonic, he said, was unacceptable. In Puerto Rico, you drink rum! He said the rum was the finest and promised they would like it. He ordered it, and was right. You could only buy that good stuff on the island, but there was a big Baccardi distillery that made huge sales on the U. S. mainland.

They found a very formal gambling casino. Lee didn't have a jacket, but it wasn't a problem. They found a jacket, which met the requiremant, with a (somewhat) matching tie.

Before returning to their guesthouse, they joined natives in the old fort area for music and dancing in the streets.

36. The Puerto Rico fort, reminder of Spanish

They learned the story of the British seige of the island back in the era of sailing. The British Navy ships had pounded the island for a long time and been repulsed. Some Catholic Nuns had staged a parade along the wall to the cathedral, with many bright torches. It was intended to boost morale. The British thought it was reinforcements and retired.

Brownie met Nell Bostwick while working on his degree at the University of Idaho. They married in April 1986 and honeymooned with a boat tour of the San Juan Islands in the Seattle area. Moscow and Pullman were only about ten miles apart, so Nell could continue her job in finance at the Agriculture Department of University of Idaho, while Brownie worked on his veterinary degree at Washington State University.

Lee's employer, GDC, sent him and Jacqueline to a one-week husband and wife management training program at the Balboa Bay Club in Newport Beach, California. This was a first-class series of meetings and group discussions that were a defining period in Lee's career.

CHAPTER 15

Commander and Mrs. Crawford

The Bolts' neighbors, Commander (CDR) Charles Crawford USN (Ret) and his wife, Agnes, were living next door when Lee and Jacqueline moved to 5155 Canterbury Drive in 1967. He had enlisted in the Navy in 1938 and became a pharmacist's mate. During World War II, he was commissioned an officer in the Medical Service Corps. He retired as a Commander, having served forty-five years and earned the Navy Bronze Star award.

Agnes was a smoker and suffered from lung congestion. Often when Jacqueline came to visit, she would notice smoke coming out of a drawer and leave to avoid fire.

After Agnes died, old shipmates often came, and Sam hit the bottle a lot. Jacqueline found old "friends" were ripping him off, taking valuable items. She became his conservator.

Jacqueline and Lee got him to go through the Naval Hospital's sobering up and alcohol prevention program. That worked for a year or so, and he fell off the wagon.

He died February 20, 1984, and was interred at El Camino Memorial Park Cemetery.

37. Jacqueline took Sam to visit relatives in Iowa

Jacqueline found Commander Crawford had designated her, his sister, and brother as heirs. She arranged the sales of the home, furnishings, and valuables. The proceeds were left to the estate. She worked with the Commander's nephew Burt to arrange the funeral and disposition of the estate valuables. Jacqueline and Lee bought many items from the estate sales. One item Lee bought was a US Navy ship's carpenter's tool chest, with most of the antique tools.

In 1984, Lee was taking a minivacation from work but getting calls from work all the time. Jacqueline told him this would keep going on if they stayed home. "We need to get away," she said. "And your parents are on a cruise to Acapulco. We can go surprise them."

Bags were packed and airplane tickets arranged. They got a room in El Faro hotel, which was near the harbor. When the ship came in, they did not see Mom and Dad get off. They took a boat to the ship, and there were the Bolts. They had a day in port and fun times.

38. Great fun in the sun at Acapulco

Clay graduated from UCSF in 1987 with a doctorate in Pharmacy (PharmD) and returned to San Diego to work for Chula Vista Hospital, near his parents.

In 1987, Lee and Jacqueline began the tradition of having about sixteen friends join them to celebrate Chinese New Year. The dinner was at the old Pekin Chop Suey House in San Diego's North Park. The tradition continued until 2018 when the owners retired.

39. Annual Chinese New Year With Friends

The restaurant had opened about 1948. Lee and Jacqueline dined there often, beginning back in the 1950s, when they lived on Boundary Street.

CHAPTER 16

England, Scotland, Wales, and France

Jacqueline and Lee made two memorable trips to England, Wales, Scotland, and France, The first in 1987 and the second in the 1990s. They had trouble separating the two, so these trips will be documented together.

They flew from San Diego to Dulles International Airport and then to Gatwick Airport, near London. It was a long but memorable flight. They were given a bottle of Dom Pérignon champagne as they departed the plane and found their prearranged lodging in downtown London. The next day was spent sightseeing in London, like Buckingham Palace, 10 Downing Street, and fighting the pigeons in Trafalgar Square.

As a car rental, they were offered a Fiat, which Lee declined in favor of a Ford Fiesta. Driving on the right side was challenging and made worse by having a standard transmission (shifting with the wrong hand). Leaving London in the late afternoon rush hour was even more challenging.

Arriving in Oxford, they found a quaint little guesthouse. The lady let them put the champagne in her refrigerator, saying, if they were late, it would be on the stairway. After an Oxford orientation drive and dinner, they returned for the champagne on the stairway.

They spent a couple of days touring the famous Oxford University, the cathedral, and the remarkably interesting shops. They went on to Exeter and Ottery St. Mary in Devonshire, simply because that was reported to be the place from which Lee's five times great-grandfather (Robert Bolt) had sailed when he was sold into servitude in the colonies for having stolen a hat in a London Public House (pub).

40. Where old Robert Bolt departed for the colonies

They found one of those beautiful Episcopalian Cathedrals in Ottery St. Mary's, and a nearby pub provided good brew and supper. They were anxious to find lodging, and a patron suggested the pub might have room. They did! It was spacious, perfect, and comfortable. No driving at all!

They went on to a guesthouse on an inlet near St. David, Wales. The evening they arrived, there were many boats anchored on the inlet between the lodging and St. David. In the morning, the inlet was dry, and boats were high and dry. What a tide range!

41. Low tide leaves the boats dry in St. David Bay

In St. David they found a lesson in British patience. The streets in town were narrow, having been laid out during horse-and-buggy days. Delivery trucks stopped in the roadway, blocking the traffic that patiently waited.

42. Refreshments in St. David, Wales

After a day around St. David, it was on to the Cotswolds and Shakespeare country. What a wonderful little piece of history! The miniatures of the area were fantastic.

Lee had trouble finding a parking place but saw many cars parked in a no-parking area. He assumed (wrongly) that they did not give tickets, but they did. There, handicapped people could park in areas designated no parking, but the placards were not visible.

The fine was paid, and they drove on to Robin Hood country. There was lots of touristy stuff in Nottingham and famous Sherwood Forest. You would think Robin Hood would pop out any minute.

Then it was on to Chesterfield and the crooked steeple on the cathedral. Next came the Scottish border, where they were welcomed by the ever-present bagpiper.

43. The Scotland greeter never rests

They passed around Edinburgh and headed on up to Sterling in Scotland for a restful night. Then they drove on to Kyle of Lochalsh to take the ferry to the Isle of Skye. There was a wonderful guesthouse, with good food. Here it must be said that the best places to eat in the British Isles are in the pubs and for breakfast the guesthouses. Unless you could find a restaurant where the chef had learned in France or Italy, you could be disappointed.

In one Scottish restaurant, Jacqueline asked the waitress, "What is haggis?" The reply was, "You don't want to know."

They toured the wonderful marshlands and waterfalls. Jacqueline was fascinated by them. All along the route when they left and went through Kyle of Lochalsh and returned to the Scottish mainland, Jacqueline had to stop for over twenty waterfalls! Back on the Scottish mainland, they went to Loch Lomond, Loch Ness (no serpent) and Inveraray to Perth, where they spent several days, going up the coast to Aberdeen and Dundee.

44. Jacqueline stops at every waterfall

Heading South, the wind was fierce. At one stop high on a hill, the wind blew Jacqueline's earrings off!

45. Old Course St. Andrews near clubhouse

46. Jacqueline remembered neighbor, CDR Crawford

In Yorkshire, they found the building where the old TV programs of All Creatures Great and Small were made in the 1980s. That TV series was part of Brownie's motivation to become a veterinarian.

47. Dr. Herriot's All Creatures Great and Small

They arrived in Carlisle and then Darlington, where they found a "jumble sale"—in American lingo, a flea market. It was cold, and Jacqueline bought a fur coat for about $14. It was great. They decided they could leave it on the way home but still have it today!

They arrived in London and found a small clean room. The next morning, they traveled to Dover and took the hovercraft (no chunnel yet) to France. Crossing the English Channel on a cushion of air was not quite as smooth as expected, but a ferryboat would have been more tumultuous.

With some help from fellow travelers, they found a conveniently located lodging with good access to the many Paris attractions. They visited Notre Dame Cathedral, the Seine River, and the beautiful waterfronts through Paris. The French were very helpful, and the food was great. Lee had always been in awe of Gustav Eiffel, who designed and built the first suspension bridge before the Eiffel Tower. Lee took extra time to walk up near the top of the Tower. Then it was back on the air cushion vehicle to England, Gatwick Airport, and the fifteen hours of flights to San Diego.

CHAPTER 17

Jacqueline's Southeast Asia Trip

In 1987, Lee's employer, GDC, was making fuselages for the DC-10, a McDonnell Douglas Aircraft. When the aircraft were purchased by a foreign airline, it was customary for the deal to include purchase of some of the country's products or services. Sales of the DC-10 to Korean Airlines included purchase of Korean travel services. The deal was that Lee's employer would fund travel by Korean Airlines, the amount of which GDC loaned. It was repaid by salary deductions. Lee could not get away from the Tomahawk program, so Jacqueline went by herself. The following is based on her notes.

OnFebruary 23, 1987 at 7:50 AM, she left San Diego for Los Angeles and the easy transfer to Korean Air. She thought this should be a "protected" flight, because as 150 members of the clergy were rerouted to a Tokyo conference. The flight left LA at noon and changed planes in Seoul, Korea and then went on to Taipei and Hong Kong.

She met Sharon Leung (tour representative) and went to Empress Hotel in Kowloon, only to feel the way into what looked like a cave, with a few flickering votive candles. It was a power outage. Sharon said she would deliver two other girls who were going to the Mandarin in Hong Kong and would check back. No way! The driver took them, and Sharon stayed.

Jacqueline went over to Shangri La (a lovely place) and drank until the electricity came on. She had never been so exhausted. Even after a long hot shower and three Advil, she could not sleep.

Up at 6:00 AM, shower again, and dressed. Out by seven to a coffee shop. Many local celebrities came in, and they were back on the tour by nine.

She hated spending two hours at the so-called jewelry factory in Aberdeen. Salespeople descend like vultures, and prices were outrageous! She left the tour in Stanley (HK), did lots of browsing, and bought ivory beads for less than half those at the "jewelry factory." Then she went back via double-decker bus and took a ferry to Kowloon.

Back at the hotel, she freshened up and went next door to the Kangaroo Club. It was a cute Australian pub. But look out. The vultures were there. She had a drink, ordered another, and turned to ask the bartender if there was a table. When she turned back around, the couple next to her were running out the door with her purse.

She screamed, ran through the door and chased them down the sidewalk, screaming and yelling. Two parking attendants also chased them. The purse was thrown down, minus passport and money. They got away. What a night with the police!

She filed a report, along with a memo to take to the American consulate to file for another passport. As soon as the consulate opened, she was on the phone. There she got a new passport in about thirty minutes. Wherever she went after that security asked why she had a passport issued un Hong Knog.

She spent the next day in a silk factory (Four Seasons) at Kaiser Estates with Darla, whom she'd met on the plane. Darla was meeting one of her partners to buy silk clothes for their silk only shop in Santa Monica. What an interesting experience—choosing, modeling, and negotiating. And there were no Chinese men involved.

Jacqueline chose a three-piece outfit. It was a day of good shopping and quality silk.

They were all exhausted so had drinks and food at La Tortilla. Darla's friend, Sean, was a really cute guy and seemed to understand the oriental mentality. He had a business there, Taipei, and one in Santa Monica. He was also a supervisor at McDonnell Douglas.

It rained all day the next day, messy and windy. They ate rice and barbecued pork at one of the stalls. There were several purchases, and she bought a linen and a crocheted top. They met cute cadets form the California Maritime Academy who were on a training cruise. Darla wanted a pitcher of margaritas, so back to La Tortilla they went. Jacqueline enjoyed San Miguel beer from New Territories Brewery. The Jade Market was interesting (watching buyers and sellers). Dinner was at a Szechuan restaurant.

March 1, she was up early, packed, had breakfast, and shopped a little. They left Hong Kong and changed planes in Bangkok, arriving in Chiang Mai at 9:15 PM. They stayed at a lovely hotel (Chiang Mai Orchid). She viewed the pool and six *wats (places of worship)* in the surrounding area.

That night, the karaoke at the Cultural Center was good. They took a minibus up to Doi Sutep. Local tribes' people were everywhere and selling everything imaginable. Jacqueline bought a cage of wild birds and let them loose! It was supposed to bring good luck—five baht! The night Bazaar was fun, supposedly the best in Thailand—good and cheap.

Jacqueline rested after a full day. Next it was the elephant farm in the morning, lunch at an open-air Thai restaurant, and then Doi Sutep Wat. She turned on TV and was sipping bourbon and water while who is on? The odd couple, Oscar and Felix, in Thailand!

48. Big elephants interacting with people

49. Watch out for that hat!

Several Russian dignitaries were at this hotel the next morning—a large delegation and police everywhere. They were at the elephant farm, and a couple of them rode elephants.

The cultural arts center show was good, but people never stopped talking. They had a Thai-style dinner. Shoes were left outside, and customers sat on the floor, eating from low, round chow tables. They had eight different foods. The Thai dancers were beautiful, but the center was so hot they had to move to an open-air theater for the tribe show.

Breakfast at the Orchid was a real treat—fresh fruits, assorted fresh juices, croissants, windmill-filled pastries, toast, cold cuts, bacon, ham, eggs any style, soups, boiled rice and rice with port, and every conceivable condiment. The service was excellent. It only took one day to master Thai coffee.

Aboard the *Royal Orchid*, waiting to take off from Bangkok, Jacqueline really did not have time to write about her experiences in this busy city. She had read in the morning paper that the Thai Air Force would be bombing along the Burmese border this morning. The Karen rebels (indigenous tribe people) appeared to be ever busy and a real thorn for both Thai and Burmese officials. There were lots of interesting stories about that area and many tribes who inhabited the area.

All air force planes finally landed. The wait was not that unpleasant. The Thais are a beautiful people, and the food was a culinary delight. These people would put American Airlines out of business, and she was traveling in *economy* class!

Clay kept her well, thanks to the Sulfa he'd given her in the send-off package. Yes, it did oxidize her tongue, but that was a small price to pay for good health.

The gringo across the aisle was coughing, hacking, blowing, taking drops, and so forth. He had wind with dinner, followed by milk—*yuk, yuk*.

They arrived in Hong Kong, where Jacqueline stayed at the Airport Meridian.

She stayed in Honolulu a couple of nights before returning to San Diego.

Brownie graduated from Washington State University in 1988 with a doctorate in veterinary medicine (DVM) and accepted a job offer at a Melbourne, Florida, veterinary practice. He and Nell moved to Melbourne, which is near Cocoa, where Jacqueline was born.

CHAPTER 18

Skiing in Idaho

Many times, during the 1980s, Lee and Jacqueline went to Idaho in the winter. Lee ensured that the grandchildren learned to ski, at Bogus Basin out of Boise or at Brundage Mountain near McCall.

50. Grandpa ensured the kids learned to ski

With Jon, Cherie, and the grandchildren, they took out snowmobiles and ranged far around trails from McCall to Cascade.

51. Snowmobiles for everyone

CHAPTER 19

Jacqueline & friends in New England

In 1988, Jacqueline, the Wattons, and other friends traveled to New York City and New England. They had a great New York visit to all the big attractions (the Empire State Building, the Statue of Liberty, the Brooklyn Bridge and all that "glitzy" harbor and waterfront). They went to a Broadway stage show or two and had lots of fun at the downtown marketplaces.

Lee happened to be on a business trip to the Naval Undersea Systems Center in Newport, Rhode Island. They met him for a brief visit and dinner and then went on up to Cape Cod and beyond. It was great to get some of that superior Lobster, rather than our West Coast langoustine that has no big claws.

52. Wow! Real Lobster! Jacqueline loved it!

They visited the Breakers Vanderbilt Estate at 44 Oche Point Avenue, as well as other fabulous homes on the famous drive.

The Boston Bay area and clothing outlets had changed a lot from when Jacqueline was living in Newport, Rhode Island. There were a lot of cheap foreign manufactured items. They did go on up to New Hampshire and Maine and briefly entered Canada.

53. There really is a Plymouth Rock

CHAPTER 20

Montgomery County (Iowa) Courthouse

In 1990, Lee and his aunt Martha Van Donge represented the Bolt family at the hundredth anniversary of the Montgomery County Courthouse in Red Oak, Iowa.

Lee's great-grandfather (Martha's grandfather), Charles Bolt, was a brick-and-mortar mason and founding member of the Red Oak Masonic Lodge. His business built most of the early brick schools and other buildings in the Red Oak area, as well as county courthouses in nearby county seats. Although he had to avoid bidding on the Montgomery County Courthouse, the company that got the contract could not finish the job. Charles took over, building the clock tower and all the roof areas. Lee and Martha represented him in the centennial celebration.

54. The hundred-year-old Montgomery County Courthouse

The courthouse represented the best design technology of the era. Iowa is extremely hot in summer. That is what brings the wonderful corn in the fields. But it can be uncomfortable to people. The courthouse was designed to take in cooler air from beneath and channel it up through the rooms. Warmed air rises out through roof vents.

The centennial committee asked for help in identifying people in pictures from the first days of the new courthouse. One was a picture of the first jury to sit in the new courthouse. Lee and Martha identified one of the jurors as Martha's father (Lee's grandfather), Benjamin Darius Bolt.

CHAPTER 21

The Bolt Sons White Water Rafting

In 1991, the Bolt crew got the annual Idaho lottery approval for August launch rights to a rafting trip on the Middle Fork of the Salmon river. In addition to the three Bolt boys, there were lifelong friends Rod Herr and Leon Scott, a friend of Jon's from Hewlett Packard, and three buddies who were seasoned rafters. They had three 14-foot self-bailing rafts. In each raft, the protocol was one rows, one fishes, and one drinks beer—in regular rotation.

The night before launch, they camped at the Boundary Creek campground below Dagger Falls. The next morning, boats were inflated and were slid down the steep Boundary Creek launch ramp to the river. Boats were loaded to await the designated launch time.

It was a lean water year. So, by mid-August, the water was very low—too low to weigh down the boats with all the supplies for the entire trip. They loaded enough for the first thirty-six hours and had the remainder flown to the Pistol Creek Airstrip about fifteen miles downriver.

Those first ten miles were rocky and tough, with lots of exiting the boats to wade, push, and drag them over and around rocks. But the fishing was terrific! Launch time was midday, and with the low water and tough work, they managed only about seven miles before stopping to camp. They were super tired after that tough rocky stuff that needed manhandling.

55. The river rafting crew ready to depart

After that first day and a half, the higher water made it much easier. They had five days to cover 105 miles, with many great sights and campsites along the way, like hot springs, sandy beaches, and tributaries flowing in. There was Harrah's Lodge at Thomas Creek (a fly-in guest-ranch owned by Harrah's of Reno and Tahoe), lots of class 4 rapids, the Flying B Ranch, petroglyphs, bears, and Rocky Mountain sheep.

56. The last four days were in challenging waters

They caught lots of good-size fish and saw more when snorkeling. They never did flip a boat, but Clay was thrown out of his boat going over a fall and was caught in the up-and-down, swirling water. He remained calm, taking in air on the upswing, and eventually "kicking out" to the stream again. Mommy's strong swimmer training paid off!

They played a game of over-the-line softball on the sandy beach at Elk Bar and turned the corner at the Main Salmon to exit at Corn Creek. After that first day, they made twenty-five miles per day.

CHAPTER 22

The Grandchildren Visits

In the early 1990s, Ryan and Jordann came to visit Lee and Jacqueline. They often went to Disneyland and Knotts Berry Farm.

57. Grandma, Ryan, and Jordann at Disneyland Flowers

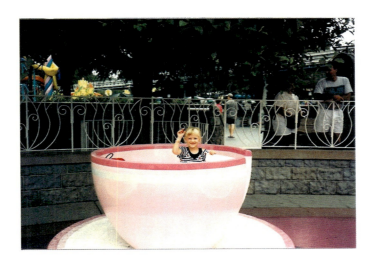

58. Jordann revolves in a Disneyland teacup

Jacqueline's brother Bill, his wife Jerry and family (Randy, Cheriiyn, Pamela, Denise, and Juanita) lived in Anaheim at the time. The Bolts visited them and had General Dynamics-sponsored open rides at Disneyland. Jacqueline's favorite ride was through the "It's a Small World" tunnel. She would emerge and get back in line to go on that boat ride to see the dancers, and hear all that music again. The Bolts also attended the Barker family weddings and parties.

CHAPTER 23

Sweeten Creek Animal and Bird Hospital

In 1992, Brownie and Nell decided to establish their own veterinary practice in a place to be chosen. Having been in the West, around Florida, and up the East Coast, they decided on the area of Asheville, North Carolina. They moved to a rental in nearby Arden, where Brownie worked as a relief veterinarian and in the animal emergency clinic. Nell got a job with University of North Carolina Asheville (UNCA). They spent lots of time determining what area of Asheville would be the best to establish their animal hospital. That turned out to be on the south end, near where they were living.

By 1994, they settled on a three and a half-acre property at 3131 and 3135 Sweeten Creek Road, with a home and a rental house. With little savings, the conversion for their use seemed doubtful. The seller agreed to carry their property purchase, and BB&T bank fully financed conversion of the rental into Sweeten Creek Animal & Bird Hospital.

Lee and Jacqueline came to help, as did Nell's father Charlie and brother Billy and Brownie and Nell's friends Bud and Sylvia Bodosky. They stripped the rental house down to load-bearing walls, ready for the contractor to rebuild to the hospital plan. Jacqueline had great fun with the garage sales that even sold odd-colored bathroom and kitchen tiles and sinks. The new animal hospital opened in January 1995.

59. Sweeten Creek Animal and Bird Hospital, 1995

CHAPTER 24

The Admiral Kidd Club Cookouts

The Navy's Admiral Kidd Officer's Club was located on San Diego Bay, just North of Shelter Island. The club began having outside cook-your-own steaks (or chicken) gatherings once a week in the summer months. When Lee had command of *Wiseman*, the pier at ADM Kidd Club was where his ship often moored. He said lots of old commanding officers at the club would kibitz the way the ships maneuvered alongside the pier. Lee and Jacqueline enjoyed going there with friends every year until the DOD stopped having many officers' clubs. It became a catering service only.

60. Cookouts at Admiral Kidd Club and bay view

CHAPTER 25

San Diego County Grand Jury

Jacqueline was appointed to the San Diego County Grand Jury in 1994. She served eighteen months, because they were converting to an annual calendar year from a fiscal year. She met and worked closely with some remarkably interesting and dedicated people.

George Foster had owned a machine shop business and usually picked up Jacqueline in the mornings and returned her home in the evening. We saw a lot of George and his wife, Avis. They had frequent social gatherings of the members, often including the grand jury presiding judge and secretary. The jurors received county citations for eighteen months of service.

61. Jacqueline's County Grand Jury certificate

CHAPTER 26

More Bolt Family Fun in San Diego

In the summer months of the 1990s, Ryan and Jordann visited Lee and Jacqueline in San Diego. There were trips to the zoo, the wild animal park, the Rubin H. Fleet Space Theater, and the beaches. The grandchildren saw the annual sandcastles competition. These events created artistic structures with big forts and castles.

62. San Diego sandcastle competition, 1994

Jacqueline took Jordann to Mister A's high-class restaurant for lunch. Parking was by valet only. The waiter addressed them by name and, they were given matchbooks imprinted "The Bolts." There were no "doggy bags," as Mister A did not send customers home with leftovers.

63. First-class lunch at Mister A's

64. Jacqueline gave Ryan tennis lessons

Of course, there were rides on the merry-go-round and model train in Balboa Park.

CHAPTER 27

Over the Mountains on Snowmobiles

Many times, during the 1990s, the Bolts gathered in Mc Call, Idaho, for skiing, snowmobiling, and other winter fun. Nearby Brundage Mountain was great skiing and snowmobiling range across the mountaintops, almost to Cascade. Young Taylor rode with Cherie and Jacqueline with Lee. It was great to see the hundreds of ice sculptures for the annual McCall Ice Festival.

65. Everybody rode the snowmobiles

66. Grandma and Jordann go too

The base of operations was Jon and Cherie's log cabin on the thirteenth fairway of the McCall Golf Course. It was great for sightseeing on snowmobiles in winter and walking to the clubhouse for golf in summer. For a time, Jon arranged for a pier and boat on the lake shore. The kids could easily fish off the pier or jump in for a swim.

The cabin was an authentic log structure with two bedrooms and a loft that could sleep eight or ten.

The big winter event in McCall was the ice festival, featuring all kinds of sculptured figures. You could drive around town (when not snowing) and see Roman or Greek figures, animals, boots, and saddles.

67. Big head sculpture—maybe Roman or Greek?

It was difficult to judge winners because of the diversity, but there were many categories. The lake was frozen, so the sculptures got full attention. In the old days, ice was cut from the lake in winter and stored in buildings filled with sawdust. During the summer, ice was dispensed from these storages all over the area. All winter, the skiing at Brundage Mountain Resort was in full operation, and Lardo's was open for dining and drinks.

68. Cowboy boot and spur

69. The big ape watches over all the festivities

CHAPTER 28

More of the Family in San Diego

The Jon and Cherie family spent some time each year in San Diego, where they learned about the beach, waves, and tides. Grandpa was always helping them build sandcastles and picking up seashells. Grandma was steering them to play tennis.

70. Snorkeling Pacific Beach

CHAPTER 29

Spain, Morocco, and Portugal

In 1992, GDC sold the Pomona Division and Tomahawk missile programs to Hughes Aircraft, and the move to Tucson, Arizona, was imminent. Lee decided it was best to retire, after his Navy career and thirty-three years with General Dynamics Corporation.

Lee and Jacqueline celebrated retirement by arranging a Trafalgar tour to Spain, Morocco, and Portugal. Their friends, Madeleine Brooks and Bert and Rena Watton were also on the tour. They flew to Madrid, where they met the guide, Gisselle, for the itinerary shown.

71. The tour explored three countries

Upon arrival at Madrid airport, it was an easy train ride to the tour's IH Hotel. The next day was busy with briefings and exploring important sites around Madrid. The country was still recovering from the dictatorship of Francisco Franco.

Lee could not forget how many of his childhood friends' families had been loyal to King Alphonso during the revolution and immigrated to the United States. Now, the country was back to a more democratic government.

72. The San Diego folks seeing the sites of Madrid!

73. Madeleine found Don Quixote

Their next stop was in Toledo, that fortress city so prominent in European history. The visit was great, but the group failed to take pictures! They moved on to Cordova, with beautiful buildings, homes, and streets and went from there to Granada and the Alhambra palace and fortress complex. It was originally constructed as a small fortress on the remains of Roman fortifications and largely ignored until the ruins were renovated and rebuilt by the conquering Moors in the mid-thirteenth century.

74. The beautiful Alhambra

Washington Irving wrote *Tales of The Alhambra*, about the history of this wonderful and beautiful place. He began with a rambling expedition from Seville to Granada in the company of a member of the Russian embassy at Madrid. The remarkable Alhambra emerged, with its courts, towers, halls, restroom, and baths. It is a wonderful treasure of the world that they were now able to appreciate even more with Irving's help.

75. Ornate and beautiful Alhambra artwork

The next stop was Torremolinos—a beautiful Mediterranean port city, close to Gibraltar. From Torremolinos, they sailed for Tangier, Morocco, where Madeleine and Grover Brooks had been married after World War 2. He was working in Morocco, and Madeleine was a secretary. She got to return!

76. The resort of Torremolinos area

77. Lee with Madeleine at Gibraltar

78. Time for a little food in Tangier

A little lunch, and they were on the bus to Rabat and Fez. Others traveled by camel. Jacqueline found a young one to pet.

79. A new mode of user-friendly transportation

In Fez, it was a bit warm, and our windows were open to cool at night. But about 5:15 a.m., the muezzin got up in his tower and gave the morning call to prayers. We closed the windows, but no more sleeping. Get up and out!

80. The souks are the places to shop, but be careful!

The bus left early for Marrakesh, where the rich and famous stage their expensive parties. You could find real first-class places to shop and play.

81. A rooftop place to relax and overlook Marrakesh

We finally got to Casablanca, a place that has really played up the movie *Casablanca,* with a much less pretentious Rick's Place. But they had the characters dressed in French uniforms, more like policemen.

82. Rick's Bar in Casablanca

The tour returned to Spain now and the beautiful city of Cordova. It was Palm Sunday. The parades were elaborate, and many floats were on heavy platforms carried by strong men under the platform and hidden. They had to change periodically to rest the men!

83. Palm Sunday Hooded Parade in Cordova

84. Palm Sunday Lady's Parade in Cordova

From Cordova, they traveled the Pacific coast and North to Lisbon. Lee had been there at the end of his first year at the U. S. Naval Academy in 1948. It was all new to the others, and Lisbon was a beauty, with the Estoril Beach and the huge castle in Sintra.

85. Lisbon port figures represent voyagers far and wide

86. Lee and Jacqueline ashore at Lisbon Portugal

The tour proceeded North to the Catholic shrine at Fatima, with the Sanctuary and the Basilicas de Nossa Senhora do Rosa and de Santissima. A suitable time was allowed for visiting or worshiping at the shrines.

In Salamanca, they found the oldest university in Europe. It was a beautiful country and city.

The tour ended back in Madrid. Madeleine Brooks and the Wattons returned home. Jacqueline and Lee continued their exploration. They took a bus to the old walled city of Avila a few miles North. It was Sunday, and they arrived before noon. The streets and tapas bars were vacant. But about noon, everyone emerged from the cathedral, and tapas and wine flowed for hours.

87. Walled fortress of Avila Sunday visit

88. After Mass, the tapas were feasts for worshipers.

They returned to Madrid and took the train to Barcelona the next day. Travel was easy by train. They could take a train from the hotel area to Barcelona and, there, find a public transit train to their hostel lodging. Emerging from the transit, they saw lots of Gaudi architecture (eyebrows over windows and flowing walls).

89. Barcelona's Gaudi architecture

The hostel was clean and neat, but they wanted a little better location and sightseeing options. The IH Hotel, like the one they had in Madrid, was too expensive. They found a fine, less pretentious hotel a block off the Ramblas, with great food nearby. They saw the Ramblas Gay Parade and toured the Columbus-themed waterfront.

90. On Barcelona's Ramblas

The train ride to Monserrat was very enjoyable. Lee had a Spanish conversation with a traveling lady and got some tips about their coming travels. They explored the area and found the main attraction was the cathedral and its shrine to the Black Saint. The shrine was high behind the cathedral altar, and the route to and from it was full of people lined up. The entry tunnel was long, and likewise, the returning tunnel.

91. Up the mountain to Monserrat

92. Black Saint Cathedral and Shrine Monserrat

Then, it was back on the lift to the train track below and return to Barcelona.

They toured the Basilica de la Sagrada Familia (Basilica of the Sacred Family)—a large unfinished Roman Catholic basilica near Barcelona, Catalonia, Spain. It was designed by Spanish/Catalan architect Antoni Gaudí. Like many historic cathedrals, it's long in the building, and not yet finished (as of 2021). On November 7, 2010, Pope Benedict XVI consecrated the church and proclaimed it a minor Basilica.

93. Sagrada Familia

The next day, they returned to Madrid and visited El Escorial or the Royal Site of San Lorenzo de El Escorial. A historical residence of the king of Spain, El Escorial is in the town of San Lorenzo de El Escorial, about twenty-eight miles northwest of Madrid. It functions as a monastery, Basilica, royal palace, pantheon, library, museum, school, and hospital. At the time of our visit, the imprints of the dictator Francisco Franco were still prominent.

The return trip to San Diego was long and uneventful, but the memories lingered long.

CHAPTER 30

Midwest Driving Tour

In 1995, Lee and Jacqueline traveled on highways to Eureka Springs, Missouri, Arkansas and through Tiler, Texas, back home. In Missouri, the decoration was "all out" for Thanksgiving, with Turkeys and wagon teams fashioned out of the farm "leftover parts."

94. Thanksgiving Turkey in Missouri

In Missouri, "old Harry" is forever remembered and honored. They visited his original home. Then a little way down the highway, they came to a river and found an enterprising citizen who had established his own business, ferrying cars from the highway across the river.

95. And horses too! What a display

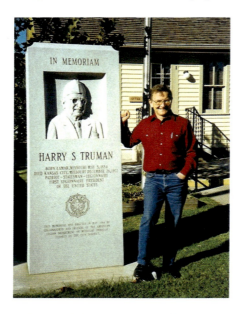

96. And old Harry is big in Missouri too

There was a long way around if you didn't want to pay the price. This was a state highway!

97. A highway privately owned and operated ferry

98. The ferry captain and Lee get us across the river

On one secondary highway, they found a huge mansion that was in poor condition, but an elderly gentleman was conducting tours for a fee. Though the furnishings and clothing were dusty and worn it was a great look at the once luxurious mansion and a view of how the obviously well-to-do occupants lived.

The Bolts joined up with Jaqueline's sister Hazel and husband, Bill Ebsary, near Eureka Springs, Arkansas. They experienced the big and famous statue of Jesus and more.

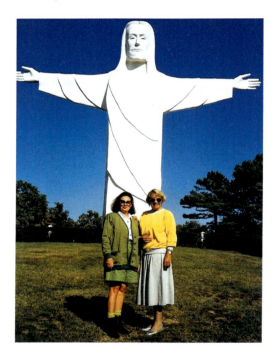

99. Hazel and Jacqueline with Eureka Springs Jesus

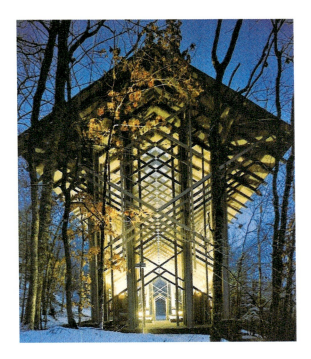

100. The famous glass Church in Missouri

The Bolts went on through Idabel, Oklahoma, to Tyler, Texas, and home. Just after leaving Idabel, they were on a two-lane highway. Lee noticed an 18-wheeler coming toward them with its right wheels off the pavement. Knowing what was coming next—a tough maneuver to get back on the road-- Lee got as far as possible to the right (wheels in gravel). And sure enough, here came the truck's trailer whipping back across the road. They made it!

Jacqueline suggested they find a bar. Lee tried to find a place to just rest, and the only alternative was a farmer's driveway, but it did allow a few minutes to recover. Then on to the next town at the Texas border. Finding lodging, they asked about a bar and dinner. It was a dry county, but the hotel had a membership club. They became members for five dollars and had martinis with dinner.

On to Tyler the next day, where they visited two of Jacqueline's brothers, Bill and Trenton, and their wives, Raye and Sandy. The next day, Sandy took Jacqueline to Dressing Gaudy and a flea market. The men and Raye played golf.

101. The Bolts in Tyler for a Barker family dinner

CHAPTER 31

Harriet and Tony Visit

In1995, Harriet, the girl who ran the Bolt home during World War II, visited Lee and Jacqueline in San Diego. Her first husband (Frank Mihara) had died, and her second husband, Tony, was with her. The Jon Bolt family was visiting, and Clay lived there, so they had a big Mexican dinner.

102. Harriet and Tony join the Bolts for a big fiesta

CHAPTER 32

Hawaii Travels Again

In the 1990s, the grandchildren were the right age to go to Hawaii. Lee and Jacqueline found the best island for everyone then was Maui—specifically the lodgings and beaches in Kihei. Of course, they had fun going up Mount Haleakala, and Clay rode a bicycle up the mountain one day. That was a workout! Lots of tourists contracted with bicycle agents to be transported to the top and bicycle down the winding highway. Few climbed it!

103. Get a load of hats and bowls in Hawaii

There they met Danny, who lived a little farther down the beach from Kihei. He made hats and baskets. He helped find good snorkeling places for the kids and helped Jon and Clay find sea turtles to swim with. Grandpa Lee, always helped the kids build sandcastles and play in the surf.

104. The big mountain is a Maui treasure

Every evening, there was a dinner, beginning with sounding the conch shell horn. There were many drives up the east coast to Hana to see the taro gardens and tropical coast. Another interesting and educational experience was the demonstrations of how life got started on these volcanic islands and became the habitat for birds.

105. Snorkeling lessons and more

CHAPTER 33

The Les Misérables Road Show

In 1995, Jacqueline's niece, Kelly Ebsary, was the innkeeper's wife in the road performance of Les Misérables on the West Coast. Lee and Jacqueline flew to Seattle, rented a car, and met Hazel and Bill. They attended the Seattle performance and took Harriet with them.

106. Harriet joins Lee and Jacqueline in Seattle for the performance

Then it was on to Portland, Oregon, and the San Francisco Bay area performances. They visited Hazel's son, Scott Lucas, in Santa Cruz and saw his remodeling of old homes.

The final West Coast performance was in Escondido, California, so the Bolts were home again.

CHAPTER 34

Texas with Trenton and Sandy

In 1995, Jacqueline and Lee met her brother Trenton and his wife, Sandy, for a business trip to South Texas and Austin. They first stopped at the Brahman cattle breeding farm of one of Trenton's friends. He said his fame was for tame Brahmans and every calf's first experience at birth was seeing him. He often waited in the area all night to make this happen.

107. Touch and see the big Brahmans

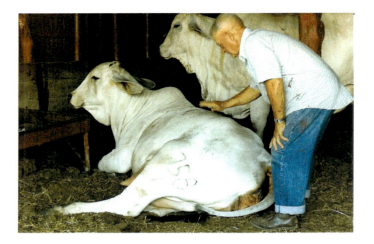

108. Big tame Brahmans

Jacqueline had a ride to be sure they were tame. They went on to Austin for Trenton's meetings and then to the deer hunting ranch where Trenton and others went hunting each year. They accompanied the deer feeding operations.

109. Not many girls have ever ridden a Brahman

CHAPTER 35

The Bolts at Pacific Beach

In 1996, Jon and Cherie brought the family to the cottages near the Pacific Beach Pier in San Diego. The family gathered every day to enjoy the sun, surf, and warmth of the waters. We had not thought about it before, but our boys grew up in San Diego, where nearly every young person was a board surfer. Jon and Clay taught themselves to use the surfboard while here at the pier. They did not take to surfing like others, but Jon did become a sea kite boarder and a kite boarder in the Idaho snow.

The Jon and Cherie family lived in a cottage on the Pacific Beach pier and enjoyed the activity, the nearby good dining, and the surf. There were always castles to build, headed by the head castle builder, Grandpa Lee. No matter where the family was, if there was a beach, he enlisted Ryan, Jordann, and Taylor for the castle building projects.

110. Pacific Beach and they get in the hot tub!

111. Building castles at Pacific Beach

112. Jon and Clay learned to surf late in life

CHAPTER 36

Back in Hawaii Again

In 1997 Lee, Jacqueline, and Clay went to Honolulu and Kauai, Hawaii. The royal palace was a great tour.

113. The king's palace, Honolulu

114. Lee and Jacqueline in Hawaii again

Kodak was still an active company, and tourists enjoyed the company-sponsored hula show.

115. The Kodak Hula Show was still beautiful

Moving on to Kauai, Clay took more scuba diving and exploration training and got scuba qualified.

116. Clay's scuba certification dives site

CHAPTER 37

Close Encounters with Wildlife

In central Idaho, there was always a winter conflict of elk eating the cattle farmer's hay. Under a government program, hay was purchased and given to cattle ranchers for distribution to the elk.

In 1997, the Bolts were able to go to the elk feeding out of Cascade. The wagons moved out to the elk territory, and the herds came to feed at the wagon. The big animals were so close you could touch them. But they had to restrain themselves because the animals may be spooked into defensive actions.

117. A large elk herd that was fed out of Cascade

118. Ryan up close to the elk as they eat

They observed their "pecking order" and poor manners!

CHAPTER 38

Brownie's Artistic and Repair Services

Brownie always had an insatiable desire to fix things and make something out of nothing. Back in his teenage years, he bought a Harley Davidson 900cc Sportster in a basket, reworked the parts, and built it into a great motorcycle. He got Jon's old Maico motorcycle fixed so he could sell it. He later made a compass in a bottle, a Teddy Roosevelt likeness, Stonehenge-style rocks, a polynesean navigation aid and more.

119. Brownie finds, fixes, and creates

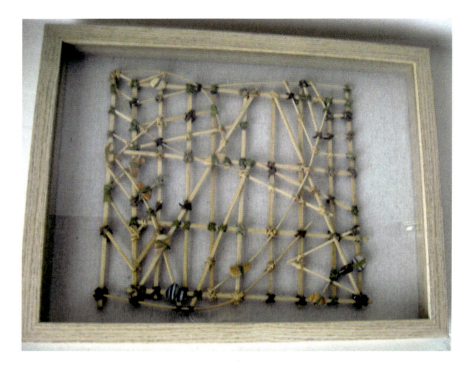

120. Polynesean Currents Navigation aid

Lee had a good office created in their 2005 remodel, and Brownie made a suitable office sign for the captain.

121. Daddy's office sign

CHAPTER 39

Memorable Turkey

In 1997, Jacqueline suggested they take a Rick Steves Best of Turkey tour. He arranged the tour through Mehlika "Mehlli" Seval, who had her own tour agency. It turned out to be the best! The twenty-five of us met at Otel Ayasofya in Istanbul, and Mehlli asked each to state why he or she had chosen Turkey. Lee said it was because Jackie told him he needed to come to Turkey.

The tour took the group through Istanbul, Ankara, Cappadocia, Cavusin, Belisirma, Guzelyurt, Konya, Antalya, Phaselis, Pamukkale, Aphrodisias, and Ephesus and ended in Kusadasi. It was a wonderful guided tour, and the final event was a stage play the tourists put on for Mehlli.

The play centered around the sultan's family, wives, harem, and staff. Jacqueline was the sultan's favorite wife. Lee was the sultan's "headhunter," tasked with getting a husband and wife to agree to have one of their sons become a eunuch in the sultan's service. One of the producers was an MD urologist!

Out in the cotton fields of central Turkey, Lee told Mehlli he bet there was only one person on their bus who had picked cotton by hand—Jacqueline. That was true, and Mehlli stopped the bus so Jacqueline could help the Turk lady pick cotton by hand.

With help from other tourists, a couple of girls developed a day-by-day account, which they published in a book that looked exactly like a *National Geographic* publication.

Although the tour ended with the stage play in Kusadasi, the group had a paid trip over to the Greek island of Samos. Jacqueline and Lee teamed with Jerry and Carolyn Wurth to tour the island by car. They went on to the island of Patmos and visited the cave where the Apostle John had written the biblical book of Revelations.

Jacqueline and Lee returned to Turkey and spent a day in Izmir. One evening, they watched *Bonanza* in Italian on Turkish TV! They next took buses to Ephesus and Canakkale and then boarded the ferry back to Istanbul. All their baggage was with them. A man posing as a porter tried to stampede people and grabbed their bags. Experienced Turkish people came to their rescue.

122. Jacqueline at the Agora in Ephesus

They returned to a hotel in Istanbul's Sultanahmet district before flying home. Lee was a bit ailing, so they were resting on a park bench. The people often stopped to talk to them, maybe just inquisitive or to practice English. This trip could not have been better.

CHAPTER 40

Hot Air Balloon Ride

In 1999, Lee and Jacqueline were visited by Jacque Burgess and her daughter, Beth. Jacque was a close friend when Lee was on his first ship (USS *Lenawee* APA-195). Jacque was the one who took Jacqueline to the NAS North Island Dispensary when her first son, Brownie, was born. Lee and Beth took a hot air balloon ride out to sea and then back over land.

123.A great tourist site, famous Hotel Del Coronado

There was a lot of uncertainty due to weather. But they landed safely, after dragging to several different sites.

124. In the gondola and ready for hot air

125. The balloon drifted out to sea and then back to land

CHAPTER 41

Maui Was the Best Island for the Kids

When Ryan, Jordann, and Taylor were old enough to handle travel, sea, and surf, Jacqueline and Lee and sometimes Brownie, Nell and Clay joined Jon and Cherie for vacation experiences in Hawaii. Having traveled the islands, the adults selected Maui as the best place to travel with the kids. They further found the best place to stay was Kihei. It was centrally located and had great beaches. They typically rented condominiums and spent most of their time at the beaches. Sometimes Lee and Ryan played golf.

126. Getting ready to swim and make sandcastles

Grandpa always got some of the kids to make castles on the beach, in such a location that the surf would eventually start eroding them. He then gave lessons on surviving the incoming surf.

127. The big mountain of Haleakala attracts all

128. Leis coming and going

In the evening, they usually had a home barbeque, with a little wine for adults. Jon usually announced dinner with the conch shell—a Hawaiian horn.

Other island points of interest included the eye of the needle and a trip to Hana and Mount Haleakala. Brownie, Jon, and Clay all swam out to sea about a mile from the beach near the fourteen-mile marker on the highway to Lahaina. They swam with the giant sea turtles.

CHAPTER 42

Italy, Germany, Austria, and a Touch of France

Lee and Jacqueline went on a tour of Italy in 1999, followed by their self-guided tour in Germany and Austria. They flew to Milan, a place of warmth and inspiration and a center of fashion, business, and wealth. They found lodging and did a self-guided tour of beautiful Milan, with its beautiful ornate cathedral and the famous opera house. Then it was on to join the tour in Varenna, a main town on Lake Como, for tour sites around Lake Como (aka Lake Lario).

129. The large and elaborate Cathedral of Milan

Lake Como is set in a landscape of rugged mountains and surrounded by calm. It's a century-old visitor attraction, with cruises to quaint villages on its shores.

The tour covered Verona's vibrant and prosperous trading center. It is said in the play *Romeo and Juliet* that Romeo climbed the wall to the balcony of Casa di Giulietta (Juliet's house). It is now a restored thirteenth-century inn. Like every tourist, Lee and Jacqueline imagined what it would be like to throw a bouquet to Romeo below.

130. Juliette's Balcony was small

The tour passed through much of the Italian countryside that was so close to Austria. One village where they spent a night was Kastelruth (or Castelrotto), a tiny village sixteen miles from Bolzano, which is a community in Southern Tyrol about fifty miles from Innsbruck, Austria. It was there that they were introduced to grappa, a strong Italian drink common in the area, but they would not drink it again. They roamed the countryside among cattle herders and dined at tiny communities accessible only by foot traffic. People wore traditional costumes. The area had more foot traffic than motor or cycle traffic.

Then it was on to Padua, an old university town with a rich history in art and architecture. Then on to Venice. The route took them through more Italian Alps. At the time, an Italian Olympic skiing champion had been Mario Tomba. As they passed through several towns, they saw signs that read "Home of Mario Tomba." And then in the next village, it was "The Real Home of Mario Tomba." Everyone wanted to get into the act!

In Venice, once an economic power of the world, they experienced her palazzi, museums, shops, hotels, and apartments. Venice convents had become centers of art restoration. They arose early one day to see the boats in action, bringing tons of fresh produce and necessities.

131. Venice parade of boats, a coordinated beauty

It was fascinating watching big boats bring in huge loads of everything the city needed and the goods being transferred into smaller boat for delivery to individual shops and homes.

Venice is also a city renowned for its early Christian mosaics. Lots of treasures to see.

The next journey was through Ravena, a city also renowned for its early Christian mosaics.

The next stop was Florence, a beautiful monument to the Renaissance and the artistic and cultural awakening of the fifteenth century. The paintings and sculptures of Dante, Petrarch, and Machiavelli made Florence one of the artistic capitals of the world. The river and its bridges were ornate, with shops lining their sides. You quickly learned not to order a martini here. If you did, you got a glass of Martini & Rossi sweet vermouth—a common Italian drink order.

132. Lee and Jacqueline with a Florence background

Then it was on to Pizza, known for its leaning tower, but also its duomo, one of the finest Pisan-Romanesque buildings in Tuscany. Its circular baptistery was a graceful counterpoint to the duomo. Everyone must see the leaning tower! When Lee took pictures here on his 1948 midshipman cruise, he was at another angle and no leaning! Trip wasted?

133. Yes. The tower is really leaning!

They had three days in the Cinque Terre, a stretch of rocky coastline on the Riviera de Levante. The area consisted of five coastal villages. Originally only accessible by sea, they had good harbors. The Bolts' lodging was in Vernazza, but they made a boat trip to Riomaggiore to experience the wonderful food and treasures.

134. Vernazza Harbor

Going farther, they were in Assisi, a beautiful medieval town with geraniums hung along the streets, great views, and fountain-splashed plazas. The basilica dominates the town as one of the great Christian shrines, which has vast numbers of pilgrims throughout the year.

135. The Shrine of Assisi

Then it was the lonesome city of Civita, a primitive suburb of Bagnoregio in the Province of Viterbo. There was only one narrow access along a footpath and bridges. It was only a 0.6-mile route in and back (a fee was added in 2013). It was primitive, but many visitors wanted to stay in the minimal ancient lodging.

136. Lonely little Civita

In the wine country, they visited Orvieto and toured the wine cellars aging wines forty feet underground. Then they went on to see Roman ruins at Paestum. There was the mozzarella cheese making facility in the cattle country. Paestum is the most important Greek site south of Naples.

137. Roman ruins at Paestum

The Greeks founded Paestum in the sixth century BC as Poseidon, which the conquering Romans renamed. It features three massive Doric temples (Hera I, Neptune, and Ceres). A museum contains extensive finds at the sites.

At Siena, the ancient history of the Palio di Siena was interesting. A bareback horse race first recorded in 1283, it is Tuscany's most celebrated festival; it occurs July 2 and August 16 each year.

138. The colorful Palio banner

The jockeys represent Siena's seventeen *contrade* (districts). Horses are chosen by lottery and are blessed at the local contrade churches. The event is preceded by days of colorful pageantry, costumes, processions, and heavy betting!

The races only last about ninety seconds each. Thousands of spectators crowd into the piazza to watch the race, and rivalry between competitors is intense. The rules of the race are very liberal, so contestants are really in a war! The winner is awarded a silk patio (banner). That banner is proudly displayed in the winner's contrade. Festivities for winner and recriminations for losers can last for weeks.

Someplace before leaving Tuscany, the Bolts had an outstanding Italian dinner in a cave restaurant thirty feet underground.

Farther south, they toured the mozzarella cheese centers. Of course, there was always the discussion of Americans saying the cheese was made from buffalo milk, and the Italians saying, in Italy, the milk comes from the cow, which is a *buffala*. Americans say buffalo, but in Italy, only the female gives milk to make the cheese.

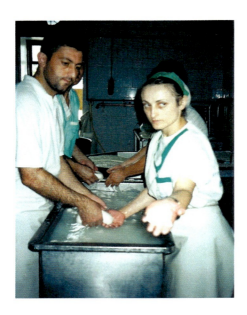

139. Making real mozzarella cheese

After tours of well-known Roman ruins, like Herculaneum and Pompei, the tour went to the beautiful Amalfi coast, Naples, and Sorrento. Pompei is the best-known ruins, with remarkable finds of streets, houses, and an amphitheater. It was the eruption of Mount Vesuvius that buried the city in AD 79.

140. Pompei Ruins, but there was so much more!

The excavation of homes revealed surprising descriptions of Roman living spaces and conditions.

141 Luxurious Amalfi Coast

The Amalfi Coast (Costiera Amalfitana) is a most visited route skirting the southern flank of Sorento's peninsula. Favorite things included dining and sipping the great wines.

In Naples, the tour dined at a restaurant that was the originator of those round dough baked pies with all kinds of stuff called a pizza. They later found at least two more restaurants that also made the origin claim.

142. Architecture of Napoli

143. Sorrento hillsides

Rome was a great historic visit. Lee had been there briefly after his first year in the US Naval Academy. He was on the USS *Macon* (CA-132) in 1948 and had one-day trips to Florence and Rome. In Rome, he had gotten a rosary and had it blessed at St. Peters, as a gift for his Catholic aunt, Hazel Collier.

144. The famous Colosseum still attracts the crowds

The traffic in Rome was fascinating. Its streets were filled with cars, trucks, motorcycles, and motorized bicycles (Vespas). There seemed to be few accidents. Lee and Jacqueline sat in a square and watched the seemingly hazardous traffic. There were "flying nuns" on Vespas and obvious tourists in panic about lanes to be in or looking to stop and collect their thoughts. Then there were the pedestrians, who do not all cross the streets at intersections. Some waited midblock until enough pedestrians joined and then cross. Despite the huge number of different vehicles, it seemed to work!

Jacqueline liked the huge Trevi Fountain and architecture.

145. Jacqueline at the Trevi Fountain

At the tour's end, they spent a day planning the journey north to Frieberg, Germany. It was a very efficient trip. Public transportation took them to the train station, where they boarded for Milan. Changing trains in Milan was easy, and they journeyed through Switzerland. Arriving in Frieberg, they found lodging and rented a car for the remainder of the trip.

Freiberg had been nearly destroyed in World War II, but by this time, the city had rebuilt, mostly in historic designs. Even a McDonald's restaurant was old style. No arches! Their *gasthaus* (guesthouse) was down near the town center, and the staff helped find the best sights to see.

The Bolts took a day trip across the border to Colmar, France, a small city with canals for many streets. It was somewhat like a little Venice. On the journey, they saw remains of the Maginot Line of French World War II defense positions.

146. McDonald's conformed to the local architecture.

Their gasthaus staff helped plan their route to Baden-Baden through the Black Forest and made a reservation for them at a gasthaus on one end of the Baden-Baden square. The Black Forest was a relaxing and enjoyable trip, through beautiful villages, with shopping and dining.

Arriving in Baden-Baden in the late afternoon, they found their gasthaus to be the best, for location and quality. There was still time to enjoy the diversity of shops in the center of town and another tasty German dinner.

147. Another wonderful historic place in Germany

They spent a couple of days in this great city, before going to the walled city of Rothenburg. There they found a museum of punishment that was frightening. Exhibits included a "rack" to stretch people, an internally spiked chamber to puncture the inhabitant, paddles for spanking, and much more. They made the evening rounds with the town security inspector, a ritual of night security performed for centuries to ensure all was well and quiet for the night.

148. Rothenburg, a walled city of great architecture

After Rothenberg, they visited several more ancient towns with great food and sites to see. Bad Mergentheim was typical, with beautiful architecture, great shopping, and helpful people. The roads were well maintained, and most people spoke English, although Lee had done his usual study of language, while Jacqueline focused on the interesting sites to visit.

149. Bad Mergentheim was the typical welcoming city

They found and toured the spectacular Neuschwanstein Castle, a nineteenth Century romantic eclecticism on a rugged hill in the village of Hohenschwangau, near Fussen. It was commissioned by King Ludwig II of Bavaria as a retreat, in honor of Richard Wagner.

150. The elaborate castle at Neuschwanstein

Before leaving Germany, they drove around Oberammergau. It was not the big visitor time of year but was still attractive and great for shopping.

Arriving in Salzburg, they visited the famous cathedral for a superior performance. Few venues could match such acoustics in the large area. People come from far and wide to experience worship and fine musicals at this cathedral.

They went on to Hallstatt, the beautiful village on the southwestern shore of Lake Hallstatter. The most surprising discovery was the burial routine. Grave plots were not assigned forever. Once interred, the "time is ticking." When the allowed time is passed, the deceased is exhumed, and the remains are disposed of in a warehouse building, with heads marked and displayed, but other bones simply piled.

151. They do not own the burial site forever!

Heading back to Munich on the autobahn was another surprise. Contrary to advertisements, traffic had been slowed, and it began to rain. It kept raining on through Salzburg and back in Germany. No cities or lodging advertising were visible from the autobahn. Lee turned off to get gas and was advised there was a gasthaus near the next exit. There, they found a great little lodging.

It was the same routine in Germany; you found nobody at the front desk but found Helga tending tables. She said they had a room and handed you a key. You looked and returned to check in, but she said, "Go move in. We will take care of that later." So, you moved in and returned to the restaurant/bar for drinks and dinner.

Lee and Jacqueline noted the huge number of names of those from this small village who had died in World War II, a reminder of the war's tremendous impact on the German people.

152. Our great gasthaus in Siegsdorf

153. Reminder of the horrible impact of World War II on Germans

Next morning, with a great breakfast, they proceeded to Munich and got a gasthaus. It was Octoberfest, but no problems—just stay out of the big busy joints. The next morning, they boarded the plane for home.

154. Ready to fly home!

CHAPTER 43

Lee's Parents

Until about 1994, Lee's parents lived and traveled a lot, but they began failing. His ninety-four-year-old father was in the hospital for near pneumonia and physically weak. Lee helped get him to do as doctors directed, and he was able to return home. At home, he still needed help, more than Fern could give. Lee interviewed and tried several girls to help them between the hours of 7:00 a.m. and 7:00 p.m., selecting Kay and Debra. Arrangements were made for Home Health to have Connie help with bathing and cleanliness.

They were doing well, and Lee helped them at tax time. Mom called in February 2000 and asked if he was coming to help with the taxes. Lee said yes and arrived in March. He told Mom he had everything ready to go to their taxman but could not find proof of payments of September and January's estimated tax.

Mom said, "I didn't pay them!"

Lee said something about penalty.

And she said, "I don't think people ninety-five and a hundred years old should have to do this stuff." In a few moments she added, "Besides, I don't think they deserve it!"

His dad had not heard this. When told, he said, "That's right! If they don't deserve it, don't send it to 'em."

Taxes complete, Lee was preparing to leave, but his dad had to be rushed to the hospital. The diagnosis was not good. He died March 18, 2000, with Lee, Jacqueline, Brownie and Nell, Clay, and Jon and Cherie and their children present. The town turned out for the Christian and Masonic funeral.

Afterward, Mom sat down at the dinner table with Lee and her niece Mary Jane. She complained of stomach pains, and lying down did not help. So, it was off to the hospital again. She had serious intestinal problems and was not in good enough condition to survive an operation. She died April 1, 2000, with everyone returning for the funeral.

They were both buried at the Emmett Public Cemetery. The many American flags remained in the yard for a couple of weeks.

155. Flags were out for the hundredth birthday and funerals.

In 2000, Jacqueline's Ponce De Leon High School class fiftieth reunion was in DeFuniak Springs, Florida. There were about sixteen attendees.

156. Ponce de Leon High 2000 Reunion of 1950

CHAPTER 44

Ethel Barker and the Farm

By January 2001, Jacqueline's mother, Ethel Barker, was living on the Florida farm, which she inherited and sold to her son, Trenton. She had been diagnosed with advanced lung cancer. The family came to help. About the same time, Trenton was diagnosed with esophageal cancer and reported to MD Anderson Cancer Center in Houston, Texas. Jacqueline and Lee packed up in San Diego and arrived at the hospital just as Trenton was being admitted and then proceeded on to the farm.

Trenton and Jacqueline's brother, Gary, had about 150 head of Texas Longhorn cattle, with which they were raising calves for sale. Lee was assigned to care for about 80 at the farm. It was winter, so there was hay to haul and feeders to move, as well as cows to change between pastures. Also, there was dragging the pasture, repairing the fence, grubbing the thistles, and fighting fire ants to be done. He had a big John Deer tractor and two smaller tractors.

157. Lee and his tractor

Sidney Perry, Jacqueline's sister Madge's husband, took care of the home grounds and garden areas, with smaller tractors and tools. Jacqueline and Madge took care of their mother, prepared the meals, and did home chores.

158. The big longhorn of Texas

Gary primarily managed the other two herds of cattle at his farm and another leased site. He helped get machinery repaired and the calves poled.

By May 21, Ethel succumbed to the cancer. Services were held, and she was laid to rest beside her husband Bunk in their plot at the Limestone Cemetery adjacent to the family farm. The land for this cemetery had been donated by Ethel's father, Henry Franklin Scott. Ethel and Bunk's son Bennis had predeceased them and was interred there.

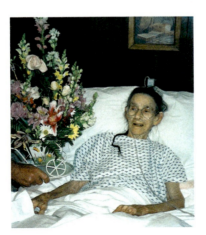

159. Ethel had flowers and a cheerful care crew

160. Ethel was interred at the Limestone Cemetery

Trenton and Gary Barker, Jacqueline's brothers, started improvements to the Barker farm, updating the old farmhouse and building a new home up at the big fishpond. This began the regular family Easter celebrations at the farm. With nine children, the Barker family was growing every year. Madge and Sidney had retired and stayed at the farm much of the time, as there were no permanent occupants living here, and they just enjoyed the farm as well.

Trenton continued to improve the farm over nineteen years, adding a new carport and laundry facilities at the original house, expanding the home (they called the cabin) at the fishpond, and building a third house behind the old home.

CHAPTER 45

Ryan and the Marine Corps

Jon and Cherie Bolt's son, Ryan M. Bolt, graduated from Boise Idaho's Capital High School in 2002 and was already committed to the U. S.Marine Corps. He and his friend Iggy reported to Marine Corps Recruit Depot in San Diego for basic training. It was intensive, and there were many challenges.

After graduation, they reported to Camp Pendleton for infantry training. The course was very demanding, but there was now time when they had liberty. Often, they came to stay a night with Lee and Jacqueline. Lee would drive them back to Camp Pendleton, and they were impressed with the salutes Lee received.

161. Ryan and Iggy on graduation day

162. Family and friends came for MCRD graduation

After infantry school, they were assigned to units. Ryan went to Kaneohe Marine Corps Air Station on the Hawaiian island of Oahu. The family came, and Ryan helped get first cottages on the base, which were particularly good for beach access. It was necessary to cross the airfield runway to enter or leave the cottages. They moved to Bellows Air Force Station, where accommodations were minimal but clean and spacious. They were away from the island's hustle and bustle. Though the beach was small and narrow, they played miniature golf and used the golf driving range and found other interests in nearby Kailua.

Ryan went on to more special security training on the East Coast. He then served several security assignments in Iraq and then on to a special unit in Afghanistan. The movie *Restrepo* was about Afghanistan operations to establish a base of that name. The base where Ryan served was the base from which Restrepo was established. He was promoted to sergeant USMC.

163. Ryan and a buddy

164. Afghanistan enroute division quarters

CHAPTER 46

Military Honor Memorials

Mount Soledad National Veteran's Memorial is one of the most unique veteran's memorials in America. It honors veterans, living or deceased, from the Revolutionary War to the War on Terror, with an image of the veteran and/or ship or unit pictures.

The memorial has stood at the height of San Diego since 1954. It has gone through many trials to be what it is today—a beacon of freedom. People are able to honor and recognize the thousands of military men and women who served and sacrificed for this country.

165. Veteran's Memorial, Mount Soledad San Diego

Lee and Jacqueline helped make this historic memorial possible with their annual contributions and by having plaques installed.

They installed a plaque honoring 4 generations of Bolts:

- 1stLt Charles Bolt, Iowa Militia during the Civil War
- Private Leland Eddy Bolt, US Army WW1
- CAPT Leland Emet Bolt, USN Korea, Viet Nam and Cold War
- Leland Emet Bolt Jr., SP4 US Army Cold War
- Ryan Mabe Bolt, Sgt., USMC Iraq and Afghanistan

166. The Mount Soledad Bolt honor service plaque

They also installed plaques honoring:

- CAPT John Phillp Cromwell USN Korea, Viet Nam, Cold War (Lee's USNA Roommate)
- CAPT Charles Virgil Wilhoit USN WW2, Viet Nam, & Cold War (Wiseman Commanding Officer)
- 1stSgt Donald Wayne Barker, US Army Korea, Viet Nam and Cold War (Jacqueline's brother).

Captain Wilhoit was commanding officer when Lee was executive officer USS *Wiseman* (DE-667) in Vietnam. His wife, Dorothy, was also a close friend. She and Jacqueline helped resolve hardships for families of deployed sailors.

First Sergeant Donald Barker was Jacqueline's brother, who upon graduation from high school enlisted in the US Army. In the infantry, he was deployed to Korea and wound up at a place called Heartbreak Ridge, where he was one of the few survivors. He changed his MOS and became a helicopter technician. Then came Vietnam, and he was again on the front lines!

The Bolts participated in various San Diego U.S Naval Academy Alumni events, like the Dark Ages Ball. While at USNA, there was a period between New Years and the spring that was cold and gloomy. It was known as the Dark Ages, and for a few years, it was celebrated in San Diego with a formal dinner dance.

167. USNA alumni celebrating Dark Ages dinner dance

CHAPTER 47

Brownie on the Memorial Serum Dogsled Run

2004, Brownie became the veterinarian on an annual dogsled run, commemorating the 1920s delivery of diphtheria serum to many Alaskan villages between Fairbanks and Nome. It was cold, like -50 degrees Fahrenheit. Much of the run was the same as the Iditarod, so the serum run had to yield where necessary.

168. The duty veterinarian on the Serum Run

The dogs were most important. At least once one was airlifted to a veterinary hospital and saved, with the news that he was saved by Brownie's actions on the scene. Brownie became a member of the commemorative Serum Run Committee, but it was later cancelled.

169. The dogs' energy delivered the serum

CHAPTER 48

Lee and Jacqueline's Remodel

In 2005, the Bolts decided to remodel their 5155 Canterbury Drive San Diego home. The home was originally a two-bedroom, one-bath home of 1,244 square feet built in 1935. The second story added two bedrooms and a bath in 1948, increasing the size to 1,844 square feet. This remodel added a loft, a dressing room, and a large walk-in closet, for a total of 2,200 square feet. The remodel retained the 1930s decor and characteristics. The revised design was developed with help of local architect Tom Silvers and the ChainTech Corporation draftsman.

170. The home before the 2005 remodel

171. With the kids gone, the house was enlarged

It will be observed that, before the remodel, there was a six-sided window in the upper story. Although obscured by a palm in the remodel picture, that six-sided figure design is reflected in a raised six-sided figure on the left of the upstairs wall.

The city said there were two historic homes within a block, and a historic survey had to be completed before they authorized the remodel. Although the city advised having a PhD historian do the survey, Lee did it. Those two nearby houses were historic because a former mayor had lived in one, and the other had been owned by the Great Gildersleeve, an old radio comic. His mistress had lived in it! The study found no famous people lived in or owned the home, and there were no unusual architectural features.

Lee and Jacqueline lived with Clay in his Oporto Court townhome for nearly six months during construction.

CHAPTER 49

The new Glynn family

Jordann Mabe Bolt's high school boyfriend was Zackery W. Glynn, a member of the Boise Church of Jesus Christ of the Latter Day Saints (LDS). The LDS religion was not new to Jordann, as her maternal grandparents had been LDS. Upon graduation, Zachery went on his mission to Mongolia. What a big challenge! Upon his return, he and Jordann planned their wedding, and were married on March 22, 2007, in the LDS Temple at Laie, Oahu, Hawaii.

172. Outside the LDS temple

173. Hawaiian wedding—leis and all

Jordann went on to complete her nursing degree at Boise State University. Zach took a different profession. He became a video designer and animator and got into that profession at DreamWorks. Their first son, Keller, was born March 19, 2009, in Orem, Utah. Their second son, Owen, was born there on January 31, 2011. Their third son, Slater, was born September 25, 2012, in San Mateo, California. DreamWorks moved the family to Southern California. And finally, it was girl! Birdie was born May 27, 2015, in Glendale, California.

The family moved to nearby Burbank, where Zach worked on the "fun stuff," and Jordann as a nurse. The family often got away to San Diego, where Jordann's grandparents (Lee and Jacqueline) and her uncle Clay lived, as well as Jordann's brothers, Taylor and Ryan.

CHAPTER 50

Nell Bostwick Brownie and Cancer Treatment

In 2008, Nell was diagnosed with breast cancer and relocated to MD Anderson Cancer Center in Houston, Texas. Lee went to Asheville and took over the veterinary hospital finances and their personal finances.

There had been delays in income tax filings. Lee drew on what his father had taught him. He worked with their CPA to reconstruct four years of Sweeten Creek Animal and Bird Hospital and personal tax reports. Brownie and Nell's friend, Bud Bodosky, was a great help in meeting Lee at the airport and taking him to the airport. He and Sylvia were also good company for a drink and dinner!

Jacqueline helped in Asheville and then went to Houston to be with Nell. Nell completed the treatments and returned to Asheville, making periodic returns to MD Anderson for follow-ups to ensure no recurrence.

Upon her return to Asheville, Nell arranged a new accounting firm for the Animal Hospital and established a quality accounting system. Lee was asked to retain the title of Chief Financial Officer.

Then Brownie had a cancerous growth in his right arm and went to MD Anderson in Houston. The treatment and surgery proved successful. He and Nell return to MD Anderson for periodic check-ups.

CHAPTER 51

Fifty-Eighth Wedding Anniversary

In 2010, Lee and Jacqueline celebrated their fifty-eighth wedding anniversary with a trip to Catalina Island. They went to Dana Point and took the ferry boat to the island. Lodging was at the Pavilion, and there was a great room with a fireplace and a private sitting area outside. Each afternoon at 5:00 p.m., wine and "pupus" were served. They toured the island and returned many times after that visit.

174. The mark of Avalon, the historic old casino

They found the golf course and stayed in various other hotels. The Catalina Canyon (now Holiday Inn) had an in-room Jacuzzi. El Galeon Bar was the favorite eating and socializing place on the Avalon Harbor waterfront. It has a great bar area and likenesses of old New Orleans jazz musicians in the rear of the bar.

175. The El Galeon Bar and Restaurant in Avalon

Jacqueline was fond the city sand sculpture on the waterfront. They only visited the Avalon Harbor and surrounding areas but found that the Catalina Island is much larger, with the two harbors; port; and much pastureland for the animals that the original developers, the Wrigley's, had preserved on the island. Further exploration was left for another time, requiring boat and vehicle transportation. Most vehicles were of the golf cart variety.

There was an airport high on the mountain above Avalon, with service to various cities in the Los Angeles area. Trenton had an instructor pilot fly his plane into and out of Avalon Airport as a learning experience before he was to later fly in this highly congested area. The Catalina Airport is a short runway, requiring practice before using.

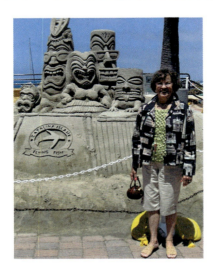

176. The Avalon Harbor sand sculpture and Jacqueline

The old-time houses were interesting and were often built on steep hillsides, with elaborate "gingerbread" architecture. There were few cars.

177. Jacqueline and the old hillside house at Avalon

Taylor Mabe Bolt graduated from Boise's Capital High School in 2010.

CHAPTER 52

Ryan and Ashlee Start their Family

Upon completion of his four-year Marine Corps enlistment in 2006, Sergeant Ryan M. Bolt USMC returned to Boise and entered Boise State University's nursing program. He received his RN degree in 2010. Upon graduation, new nurses were rarely hired directly by a major Hospital. However, Grandpa Lee, found that Naval Hospital San Diego sometimes hired directly upon graduation, and Ryan was hired after a telephone interview. His initial assignment was in the maternity ward, and then he later moved to the emergency center.

Ryan had met Ashlee Deninger while at Boise State. Upon graduation, Ashlee got a job in San Diego at Sharp Psychological Care Center. They announced their engagement at a dinner in 2012.

Ryan Mabe Bolt married Ashlee Deninger on August 5, 2013, aboard the *Electra*, a yacht operating out of Marina Del Rey, California. It was an elaborate ceremony, preceded by a pre-wedding frolic at a pier-side bar. All Jon and Cherie's family and Ashlee's parents, plus Lee, Clay and Jacqueline, were there.

178. The party yacht

Zachery and Jordann Glynn brought their three boys and were fun to watch at their first wedding experience. The bride's father, John Deninger, placed the traditional garter on Ashlee's leg.

179. The wedding party

180. Newlyweds

The cake was a beautiful two-deck round, with a figure of the groom sweeping the bride off her feet.

The yacht *Electra* got underway for the ceremony at sea and then the return to port with music, food, and a dance program. Of course, the drinking had been going on since the party came aboard.

181. The cake, with the groom sweeping the bride off her feet

CHAPTER 53

Kensington Celebrations and Events

The Kensington area, where Lee and Jacqueline lived since 1967, had its own local parades on Veteran's Day. After a US Army tank damaged a street, it was changed to holiday at home, with a largely family parade. Several times, the Good Times Inc. that Jacqueline, Joy Woodward and Gay Woods initiated had a truck float in this parade. Rene Woodward provided the truck. The parade featured random local activities, like school and club bands, old cars, and dancers. Later, things just happened, like the neighborhood bar that passed down the streets in 2013.

182. The Kensington mobile bar just appeared one day!

CHAPTER 54

More Time in Hawaii

Lee and Jaqueline traveled to Hawaii once or twice a year after 2010, usually staying at the Hale Koa military hotel on Oahu's Waikiki Beach. It was near great shopping and has great accommodations, with weekly offerings of a luau and comedy, magic, and music shows. There were many great restaurants within easy walking distance, and the pools and beach areas were in a tropical paradise setting.

During every Hawaii trip, Lee and Jaqueline went to the Pearl Harbor Base World War II memorial and to the Punchbowl Military Cemetery.

Each evening. it was a treat to go to the Warrior's Lounge for drinks. They renewed visits with the Kims and Wards, acquaintances from the days when the husbands were aboard USS *Lenawee* (APA-195). Jacqueline traveled well and enjoyed the variety.

CHAPTER 55

The Last Chinese New Year Celebration

In 2017, Jacqueline and Lee staged the last of their annual Chinese New Year Celebrations at Pekin Café in San Diego's North Park area. There were fifteen guests. The Lion Dance, the food, and the decorations were spectacular. The restaurant closed after the celebration.

CHAPTER 56

The Admiral Baker Golf Club

Lee had begun playing golf before retiring from General Dynamics in 1992. He'd joined the Admiral Baker Navy Golf Cub back when the clubhouse was in a small temporary building leftover from World War II. By 2000, the new clubhouse, bar, and restaurant had been built, and the Bolts had many friends there. They came there most evenings.

Jacqueline had a big ninetieth birthday party for Lee in 2018 at the ADM Baker Golf Cub, with over a hundred family members, neighbors, and friends. There was food, music, and drinks. The big surprise was when their club friend Eddie, who had played previously with the Beach Boys, offered to play his drums. He was a big hit, particularly with Zach and Jordann's boys. They joined in dancing!

CHAPTER 57

Jacqueline's Memory

About 2010 Jacqueline began having memory difficulties, like trouble finding her way home. She was referred to Dr. Evans of UCSD Medical Center, who found indications of Alzheimer's disease. By that time, the couple was going most places together, and Lee took over the driving. They traveled frequently to nearby places in California and Arizona and then across country to the Barker Farm in Florida or North to Idaho. They later flew those greater distances.

Flying was a challenge getting through the TSA inspections. Jacqueline always wore earrings, bracelets, rings, and necklaces. Lee gave up trying to get her to put it all in a sack until after TSA. She considered that not being dressed, so Lee waited patiently. She was a great traveler.

In 2020, the Chinese virus (COVID-19) lockdowns cut travel and sentenced them to virtual house arrest. All Jacqueline's stress "came to a head" in July 2020, when she became combative and was taken to the memory care unit at UCSD Medical Center Emergency Room. She was released to Stellar Care, a nursing home, where she could receive care and be seen by a doctor every week to be stabilized and cared for. Visitation was initially allowed every two weeks under distancing rules. Eventually all residents received the Moderna COVID-19 vaccination, and more frequent visiting allowed. She continued to degrade and passed away March 29, 2021. She did not die *of* COVID-19! She died because of it!

Lee arranged San Diego Mortuary services and transportation to DeFuniak Springs, Florida. With the assistance of a local mortuary and Bishop Miller of St. Agatha's Episcopal Church, Jacqueline was placed in Limestone Cemetery at her family's farm the day after Easter. It was perfect timing, as Easter marked her family's traditional meeting at the farm. Since Jacqueline was one of nine children, the family was a lot of people.

Jacqueline was always well dressed in the latest fashions and a joy to be around. She loved parties and could get one started on short notice. She gave life and guidance to three boys—a veterinarian, a HP project engineer, and a clinical pharmacist. They are strong swimmers and learned to tap dance!

183. At the Kensington holiday at home 2019

It is up to the newest family members to carry on Jacqueline's rich legacy of motivation, instruction, and life experiences.

184. Keller, Owen, Slater, and Birdie Glynn

185. Leo Bolt, the newest great-grandchild

ABOUT THE AUTHOR

Captain Leland Emet "Lee" Bolt (US Navy, retired) was born in Payette, Idaho, on August 30, 1928, and grew up in nearby Emmett. He graduated from the US Naval Academy in 1951 and served on USS *Lenawee* (APA-195), on USS *Princeton* (CVA-37), at US Fleet Gunnery School San Diego, and on USS *Uhlmann* (DD-687). While serving in the Naval Reserve, he was recalled to active Navy duty several times. He was a member of the engineering department at divisions of General Dynamics Corporation for thirty-three years. In 1975, he earned his MS in Systems Management from University of Southern California.

Lee's memberships include associate fellow in the American Institute of Aeronautics and Astronautics (AIAA), National Genealogical Society, US Naval Institute, Military Officers Association of America (MOAA), Association of the US Navy and USS *Midway* Museum.

Lee wrote *Leland & Fern Bolt Heritage: Family, Business and City Service* about his parents and associated ancestor history.

ABOUT THE BOOK

This book is in honor of Jacqueline Bolt. She was born Jacqueline Joyce Barker in Cocoa, Florida, and grew up in the Florida Panhandle. Leland Emet (Lee) Bolt, the author, was born in Payette, Idaho. It was a wonder they even met. This is the story of their family, history, and travels.

Jacqueline's sister, Hazel, was married to a Naval Officer, who was executive officer of the navy torpedo station in Newport, Rhode Island. While Jacqueline was visiting in July 1950, Lee was assigned a ship home ported in Newport and met Jacqueline. He knew this was the girl for him, and by Christmas, they were engaged. They married in 1952.

Jacqueline was the most wonderful wife and mother. She was the guiding light when Lee was away on deployments (Korea and Vietnam), operational commitments, and business trips. She closely monitored the boys' school curriculum and work. She taught them respect and manners. Says Lee, "Our children and I are so thankful that this wonderful girl was a loving strong example and guiding parent. She ensured that the boys became strong swimmers and could tap dance!"